MW01206134

Redwood Writers
2023 Poetry Anthology
Including the Poets of California Writers Club

PHASES

Les Bernstein and Fran Claggett-Holland
Editors

Jory Bellsey, Skye Blaine,
Simona Carini and Margaret Rooney
Editorial Assistants

An anthology of poetry
by Redwood Writers
A branch of the
California Writers Club

Redwood Writers 2023 Poetry Anthology:
Phases

Editors:
Les Bernstein and Fran Claggett-Holland

© 2023 by Redwood Writers

ISBN: 979-8-9853503-3-3

Library of Congress Control Number: 2023911316

Book design
by Jo-Anne Rosen
Wordrunner Publishing Services

Cover art: "Spirit Rises"
by Sherrie Lovler

Published by Redwood Writers Press
PO Box 4687
Santa Rosa, California 95402

REDWOOD
WRITERS
PRESS

Contents

Appendices

Introduction

Dear Reader,

Just as the moon waxes and wanes, in these pages you will find flows of emotion, celebrations of the quotidian and an equanimity that can be found in ever-changing phases of existence. This anthology showcases a diversity of poetic expression from a tapestry of poetic voices.

The poems in the anthology offer a touchstone through the various phases life weaves. In Phases you will encounter a delicate dance expressed with love, loss, introspection, optimism and of course humor (dark and light).

I am deeply grateful to the talented poets who have contributed their work to this anthology. These poems serve as a testament to the power of poetry to inspire, heal and unite us in the mysterious predicament of what it is to be human.

Welcome to *Phases*.

All the best,
Les

Acknowledgements

The Redwood Writers who have made this book possible are, of course, the poets. Without them, there would not be this anthology. It takes courage to submit poems and face possible rejection.

In addition, we want to acknowledge and thank the following members:

Our dedicated editorial assistants: Jory Bellsey, Skye Blaine, Simona Carini and Margaret Rooney

Our book designer: Jo-Anne Rosen

Our cover artist, poet and friend: Sherrie Lovler

and our gratitude to the Redwood Writers Board of Directors for supporting this project.

Contest Winners

Kate Adams
San Francisco Peninsula Branch

Snowfall

Wet earth clings to your boots.
I remember weather harsher than this,
clouded, like your eyes,
temperatures hovering
at the freezing point. You
squint, stare at a ridge of trees,
their naked calligraphy
against the sky.

What you did to me
I never told, only wrapped
my scarf tighter, walked the streets
down to the river. My pockets heavy
with books, scraps of paper, pens,
I let the water sink, blue and silken,
into my empty bones.

Wet earth, the browns and blacks
of late winter, arthritic branches budding
at their tips. Your boots
sit in the kitchen, wiped clean.
You open a window, breathe
the falling air. All around you
seems dulled, dead, waiting.
I move toward you, touch your arm.

You turn, your dark eyes take me
in, old skies. I remember
other weather, storms

I'm shuttered against still—
Your eyes catch the light, you laugh.
Under this late snow, hard bodies
soften. I feel them letting go.

Dana Rodney
Redwood Writers Branch

Letter to a Childhood Friend

As for me
I am living tucked away
beside a forgotten vineyard
the vines grown shaggy and fruitless
misshapen
thirsty for attention.

You are right, my old friend
we know nothing of ourselves
our bodies age like withered grapes
still clinging to the vine
while our minds continue asking
the questions of children
the answers always begging more questions
until we give up asking.

How about you, old friend?
Remember when we inhabited bodies
that sparked like fireflies
and our dreams rang out like church bells?
Remember when we thought life would answer us?

I feel as if I am ever trying
to gather up the years in my arms
like a great bundle of dry leaves
but the more I pick up
the more fall from my grasp
until I have given up entirely
and let them all blow away in a spiral wind.

And you
have you come to terms with the years?
or like me
is the core of you
the green apple core of you
still staring in wonder

at a broken sparrow's egg
or a cluster of ripe berries
in a brambly wood?

Mark Meierding
Redwood Writers Branch

Late Summer in California Hills

Over eroded gullies,
fence posts dangle from barbed wire
like dead marionettes.
Coming down from the mountains,
coasting around the next bend can seem like
scouring out an endless olla.
After one more white mile marker
you pull over…
possibly to break the slumbering spiral of brown pigments.
Engine silenced. Key disengaged.

Emerging out of interior's cool bath
to an affront of heat,
where fragmented scents catch like burrs on disquieted wind.
A quality indistinct, yet familiar,
a slightly sweet tincture,
or wildfire somewhere east, but no tan cloud squats on the
    horizon,
at least that you can see.

Native sage or santolina,
if you could nail down the aroma,
wouldn't surprise you,
but this comes tinged with fermentation, as if
in the abandoned orchard of a distant arroyo,
fallen crab apples lie ungathered.

In this place, mindfulness is already dry,
bark peeling off pepper trees.

Perhaps the season's last rattle of heat
makes decay even in waterless matter.
Perhaps what you smell
is the smoldering culmination of a lengthy fast.

A Shakespearean Apology

My fear, again, has birthed an ugly child
While you retreat to nurse a bitter gut
And I, adrift on waves that toss me wild
Pray that our precious love I have not cut
How may I calm this frightened fiend within
That takes me by surprise and steals my tongue
My goodness yanked below the roots of sin
Where songs of deepest trust remain unsung
Such presence true, love's gift I've rarely known
Yet quick am I to question and to doubt
May courage risk my heart to all we've sown
And grow our cleansing sage, even in drought

It is forgiveness that I ask for here
Committing kindness to replacing fear

Pamela Singer
Redwood Writers Branch

Too Much Time in the City

I've been too long in the city.
Streets, avenues, highways.
No animals have spoken to me.

This morning I don't recognize the sun.
I leave streets that run perpendicular to the sky.
Cars, buses, incessant flashing colors.

Return to my home near the river.
Sandy banks transformed by storms,
compact and silent as snow
and the slow, steady rhythm of river sliding to sea.

Not far from here, ocean calls.
Here where I am not far from the sea.
Tonight I will hear owls
and the sky tumble backwards.

Megan McDonald
San Francisco Peninsula Branch

Burn Scar, Lake Margaret Trail, Alpine County, California

I weep for
What the heat
Has done
To your skin
Light brown
Living bark
Licked black
By wild flames
Your textures
Turned to char
And dust
Your pulp
Seared and
Cauterized
So you will
Never again
Pull water
From the earth
Your limbs
Snap like bones
Your sap seeps
To the surface
Drawn outward
By tenacious fire
It ran and crackled
Scenting
The mountains
With your

Evergreen tears
Mine taste
More like
Phantom smoke

Pamela Singer
Redwood Writers Branch

Green Light

I.

With astounding clarity, I chose one man to love.
Met in rays of green light.
Voices echoed in twilights deeper than bones.
Skimmed celadon rivers, legs wrapped
around each other, bison charging the moon.

II.

Storms of words sank into earth dark as lies.
Grass we once lay on, brown from canceled suns,
and fire moons that strangled blistered grass.
Left for different countries in different worlds.

III.

There is the garden.
Broccoli's green florets.
Zucchini's green tongues lick soil.
Green beans occlude the trellis they climb.
Oregano, dill, thyme, green on the tongue.

Green apple swollen with emeralds in a child's palm,
juice surprising her with silk and satin.
Hidden by branches, chartreuse pears.
Verdant grapes on fingertips.

IV.

At dusk, a man plants flowers, turns the sky teal.
Broad fingers and hands transform soil

into rich loam with manure and seaweed.
Woman cans tomatoes' rich flavors.
Strong hands lift jars from boiling water.
Her loose melon breasts and abdomen covered in a checked apron.

Stares out the window at changing seasons,
emerald summer to ruby autumn.
This in-between time, late summer, early fall
when everything is alive, hums and whispers
in varying shades of brilliance into kaleidoscopic dawn.

Wayward Angel

I float face up in the pool
suspended
arms splayed like a crucifix
a hummingbird flits over me
a jet intersects thirty thousand feet above
Is that not a miracle? and me, floating?

What awful joy is life
what inconsolable beauty
eight billion crashing souls
spilling hailstorms of words
we pace ahead of ourselves irreverent, strident beings
imagining ourselves deserving
when
the depth of forgiveness we owe
each other is
withheld.

And you
(there is always a you)
who didn't love enough
who didn't give enough
but floating here I realize
it was I
who held too tightly to my heart.

How can I contain it all?
the pleading animal eyes
the disappointed lovers
the barely cloaked resentments of children
the barking foxes
the wild finches
the night-blooming jasmine.

The universe screams inside me

We clash like sparks of God
flinting off each other
floating like wayward angels
in an infinite storm of be.

PHASES

Our Seasons: A Hoosier Romance for Carole

If I loved you when the dogwoods were in blossom
And their silky petals floated to the ground.

If I loved you when the bees romanced wild roses
And the morning glories slipped their sleeping gowns.

If I loved you when the maples flamed to crimson,
Then their scarlet leaves succumbed to autumn's pall.

If I've loved you in the passion of these seasons,
Now when snowflakes fall I love you most of all.

Waking Up With a Spider in My Ear

My nights have been stripped of all shelter
no moon ushering passage into liquid light
just an old thirst for deep voyage
stowed away in the barracks
of my dreamless life.

Something wandered
through my nakedness last night
rummaged through my vacant corridors
unanswered riddles
crawled into the barracks
of my barren dreams

was it trying to weave
the threads
of a new story?

I was half-born into morning
pushed forth by what I felt
but could not hear -
the terror of no answers
the certainty of no arrivals
only tiny remnants of a spider
crushed in my ear
after its deadly voyage

vanquished and lost
in the labyrinth of my longings
the dream-weaver had left me
only one sign,
the smallest of threads
to find my way back
into morning.

Fallacy

Inside the core
of all hard things
lies hidden
its other self
perhaps softer, gentler
more fragile

the boulder perched
on the stillness
of a marbled sky
does it not hold
the transient journey
of a speck of sand?

or the glacier forged
into colossal ice
does it not bear
the weightless dance
of a fleck of snow?

even under the bedrock
of our firmest convictions
lie the brittle membranes
of our other self
holding onto the fallacy
that all things solid
be it matter, be it love
will forever be unbreakable

is it the terror of morphing
into nothingness

that blinds us to the alchemy
of our own fragility
or the insatiable hunger for certainty
that harbors fallacy
as our only shelter?

I too believed our love
was unbreakable
now
as I hold the pieces
of every truth that shattered
in the making of ourselves
as I see
the fallacies we embraced
to make love possible,
I touch the lingering dust
of your absence
the rock-solid suspicion
that no matter how hard
how certain
how beautiful,
nothing remains unbreakable

El Salvador

Santa Marta, 1988

There are moments that linger
in a rhapsody of silent breaths
all knowing in the distance of time
as if dying and living
shared the same beauty
death and poetry blossomed
from the same root.

The morning the army helicopters
thundered through the village
I took my last breath
circled the lines of my life
like a top spinning
its last rounds,
the hand that held my fear
was a boy's
a tiny clump of fingers
tutored by war
on the stillness of surrender.

Stretched out on a field of white flowers
our muted bodies readied
for the helicopters' blast
the boy picked a clump of petals
cupped them in his hands
gave me to smell
their tiny burst of life,
tranquil
he placed them in my pocket
like a concealed truce

he had reached with time
his index finger motioned for silence
and the scent of peril drowned
in the softness of the moment
he chose to see.

Who had taught this child
the quiet scent of serenity
the beauty with which life
conquers death in one
sudden moment
its petals guarded
like tiny saviors
in god's little hands?

I asked then
(and I shall always keep asking)
as I search
in my hollow pockets
for a life to hold
and a distant scent of petals
lingers
still stranger to fear
gifting me
with only one moment,
to hold not
but to surrender.

Seen One Bird . . . Seen 'em All

Tell me   then
which bird you mean
this *one bird* you say you've seen

duller than a dirt clod
forgettable as fog   did it flash
a flaming crest and thorny claw

sleek as a coronation boot
or drenched and disheveled
ravenous beggar on your doorstep

did it slip you a shiny silver earring
or a pull tab from a beer can for your troubles
stolen baubles on your window ledges

was it the Phoenix of myth ascendant
or Harpy with a female face
did it grace you with a song

perhaps you were the first layman
to spot the Quetzal   elusive and
resplendent resident of the tropics

just the tail   I'd guess
draped like a shimmering shawl
from the tree hole of a noble palm

so now   my fellow traveler
weighted with ennui
what's next for you~

Seen one flower . . .
Seen one lover...
Seen one poem . . .

Seen 'em all ?!

Homage to Comfort

We are the soft shirts
squandering our Julys in the depths of
a wicker basket in the guest room closet
awaiting our annual summons to

a late night vigil on the deck
when the sky is stroked with shooting stars
the fabled Perseid showers of August
the mystical discourse of Great Horned owls

We are the flannels your skins are craving
not the straight-laced bind and frill
We cuddle you at hip and bosom
nuzzle your chilly collar bones

Look how we wear our trade
dabs of caulk where cufflinks go
a swatch of lemongrass (or was it oyster)
a smear of roofing tar along the tails

Pragmatic we are to the final thread
Check out our buffalo plaids
primary red on candid white
loyal blue on wistful gray

Shoulder to shoulder
sleeve over sleeve
we breathe with the breeze
on the backyard clothesline

casually   lustily
out in the open
we dance
we dance
we dance

Merge Lane

Is there a merge lane between life and death?
passing allowed to the right or left?
racing to the end
gritting, grinding, preparing to leap
some days cruising on autopilot, half asleep
meandering, distracted
small moments missed, life redacted
omens etched in faint outlines
breathing between the lines
wheels keep turning
adding losses to yearning
cling or let go,
now approaching the end of the road
ready or not
here I go

Continuous Melody

When I was sixteen, I swooned
over stories of lovers who reconciled
at a windy road's end. The pain
was worth the rapture I breathed
heavily into dog-eared pages.
Then I met you. And I knew I couldn't
drift away even for a roaring comeback
like vinyl's continuous melody.
The hand that pulls me in nightmares
from flight's rubble, sinister shadows
is yours. I recognize the touch
in the disintegrating dream and wonder
when did I weave you in? Or does my REM
spool from our subconscious commune?
Marriage softens personas like throw pillows,
potted plants for houses. Yet you remain
unembellished as unbuttered toast
I savor with black coffee. Every crusty
bite tastes of pliable dough, porous
as the soil which lets roots grow
deep and nourish from new places.

The Summer of Staying Put

October 2020

It was the summer of staying put,
Meeting our flora on endless walks.
Measured breaths behind the mask.
The summer we taught our eyes to talk.

Beaches sprawled with uncluttered view.
Amusement parks gathered rust.
Hair grew out like summer of love.
Neighborhood joints went quietly bust.

Tactile senses hit the snooze.
We used the network's every bit.
Sourdough starter and stubborn seeds
Became our emotional conduits.

Leaves are turning their first blush,
Days shorter, peach twilight.
I pine for times of flying over oceans,
Hugging my parents with more than sight.

Just This One

Ain't no such thing, she said,
smoothing her flour sack print apron
over her wide knees.
Ain't no such thing at all,
bein' as how
we're all made out of dust and space—
us and the trees and the dogs
and the stars—
all made of tiny specks
with space around them.
Mostly space, that's right.

She kicked the floorboards
with her toe, making
the old porch swing's chains
squeak as it moved.
I curled up content under the fat
of her upper arm,
my skinny girl arm tucked around her,
and watched the swirl
of tiny bugs in the porch light's halo.

A separate reality?
Ain't no such thing, she said,
patting me.
Just this one here.

Minus More

Tick tick tick
seconds minutes hours
days weeks years
expire
never to be reclaimed
once a mighty glacier
now slowly melting away

I am minus now
less of everything
rendered irrelevant
nostalgic
reminded of
what was once
more

A life
fleeting
like time lapsed video
truncated
into a single breath
a blink of an eye
a random thought
vanishing in an instant

Once there was more
time
dreams
growth
learning
all additions

Now I am minus more
subtracting
erasing memories and time
morphing into something
unrecognizable
shrinking
in every way

I am more minus now
listening and waiting
for each tick tick tick
watching and hearing
an ever-present
clock

Just Another Day

My irritations
never grow into pearls
they are more like sand
in my eye
annoying persistent

irritation 1
I rinse my eye with an eye cup
full of solution
over and over as if
I am toasting to the queen
resigned to the annoyance
I start focusing on the next thing

irritation 2
A thread in my sock
has gotten caught
on the sharp edge
of my pinky toe nail

irritation 3
After squeezing into
3 different pair of pants
each more suffocating than the last
I curse myself
for gaining weight not exercising
then settling on sweatpants

irritation 4
Shoes congruous with sweatpants
hikers will work nicely

several pair tried
none are comfortable
why after all my years
would a bunion start budding
on the top of my right foot

irritation 5
Where are my keys and wallet
10 20 30 minutes searching
I pass the hall mirror
notice my face is bright red
like a balloon over inflated
ready to explode
needing some air to calm myself
I go outside and sit on my porch
feeling the sun's warmth
on my face
I begin to settle
relax

It's then I realize
I locked myself out of the house
my eye no longer bothers me
I am not thinking about
my sharp pinky toe nail
the beginnings of a bunion
the snugness squeezing my stomach

yes
 it is only just another day

Blazing Times at Spring Lake

The hard heel of July, dry
as week-old sourdough. Lake
a bowl of winter's enduring rain
all that rises from below.

Night Heron hunts in the shallows.
April's mud dried to ruts. Reeds.
Blue Chicory, Yellow Deer Lotus.
Bewick's Wrens. Black Phoebes.

When the trail veers down to follow
the water, I bend with it into shadows
of live oak and willow. Geese
honk their way to a watery landing.

Birds have their songs of settlement.
Chirps of the crowd, crows yakking.
Open-mouthed cries of hatchlings.
Soft clucked check-ins with mates.

Nothing like us in these blazing times.
Is there more in that lake's glimmered
surface than frogs or fish? Heron knows
the nature of hunger, how need gnaws the gut
unwilling to be ignored.

Solastalgia

a family gathers smiling
in this photo not yet sepia
someone not yet missing
a routine document
of ebb and flow

we had wax wings
a common metaphor
of earnest self-importance
grand and vague
yet melting near a cold star

in a solitary confinement of self
and far off country of dream
I think I keep seeing you
I see you everywhere

what is past remains past
my heart is on the outside
how can I be homesick
while being home

Before Begatting Began

with all its howling mistakes
and some sublimity intact
the repetition of existence
with its generalities
and its particulars
shuffles along

trued by circumstance
a paucity of perspective
with sure-footed uncertainty
creates faulty assumptions
makes conviction almost reliable

unanswerable questions linger
enter the vestibule of belief
before begat begat begat
the big bang?
are you sure

Yahrzeit

it is your day today
I leave the windows closed
and watch the leaves scatter
and remember the sun

I know the moment
time slithered away
that day unlike all others
tangling into a hard knot

I will light a candle
to chaperone my way
to toggle between
here and nowhere

it is winter again
you inhabit the wind
while terrestrial business
continues
as if nothing changed

Ten Tenets for the Best You

I:

Embrace
embracing mistakes you'll learn three things what should've worked
what could've worked
what didn't work
now you know

II:

Know
you can't control what happens
but you can control your reaction to it
what should've happened
what could've happened
what didn't happen
doesn't matter

III:

Love hard
its safe
what should you love
what could you love
what didn't you love
go hard to love

IV:

Be
your own validation
ask yourself
what should be validated
what could be validated
what wasn't validated

and does it even matter
do not compromise yourself

V:
Take
your attention off yourself
look outside yourself, see what's needed
try to provide it
what should you do
what could you do
what will you do
it matters

VI:
Feel
free to live kindness
what should you care for
what could you care for
what will you care for
be like a love bug

VII:
Know
that everything alive wants to survive
what should you nurture
what could you nurture
what will you nurture
be gentle with the world

VIII:
Dare
to be great
march to your own inner drum
what should you create
what could you create
what will you create

don't be afraid
of uncharted territories

IX:

Allow
yourself to experience
all that life presents
don't suppress
love
pain
laughter
grief
"it's life and life only"
let it move on through

X:

Be
present

Papa

I always loved the end
the end of a school day
the end of a chapter
the end of a year
the end of dinner
it always meant
something special followed

as I grew up
the end meant goodbye
goodbye to people I would never see again
goodbye to characters I loved
goodbye to another 12 months
goodbye to the peas and carrots that sat on my plate
but the special that followed
became a bitter taste

it no longer meant time with you
no cookies
no pretzels
no games of Jenga
no bucky ball

memories bridged with sentiment
escape in a tangled knot
reminiscing is the first ripple
of our end's sinking stone

monastery

1986

olivewood beads
handwoven shawl
reflection journal
unpacked with care
ten silent days
ten days alone
the hours loom

every day
old graveyard walk
I trace the dates
on worn-down stones
died at eighteen
twenty-two, our angel
taken at birth

on the way back
I dodge rushing cars,
horns, anxious people
who have no notion
the breadth of a day
minute by minute
in silence

how still the chapel,
sacred names
on the breath
fingering the beads
1001 times
again
and again

camaraderie

June 1976

hunched on a hard chair
in an airless room,
I cupped my head
in my hands and wept

to save his life
they would saw
through his breastbone,
his chest as small
as my open hand—
stop his heart,
rebuild the inside
staple him shut

a presence beside me,
her hand a mere moth
dusting my arm, said
here—for you
offering a fresh-lit
Marlboro bearing
her kiss of lipstick
I accepted the gift

glancing up, four
others, all mothers,
waited
us, too, one said

moon bathing

rare as an oriole sighting
late-night soaks
in full moonlight
warm steam rising
a delicious seduction

when my fingers
become raisins
I climb out of the tub
into the nip of night's chill
wrap in my fleece robe
pull up the hood
to keep the heat close
to claim moonlight's touch

bathed in its grace
I slide under the covers
offer up prayers
and slip into deep sleep
that kiss of night
in the tenderest light
marks and heals me

Beyond My Voice

Words wrap around my mind
drum loudly in my head
like a pileated woodpecker
hammering holes in bark.
But no rhyme or rhythm
comes as clear as walks through woodland
or the pelt and fury of rain.

I toss stones in Asbury Creek
wander among wildflowers and coyote brush.
Two red-tailed hawks mate
and common crows take flight.
Creatures come and go
beyond my voice
obeying only spring.

Covid Blues

What is it, Doc, I just can't shake these blues,
That have infected me from scalp to shoes.
I've got no energy to kick this funk.
I've been reduced to just one shriveled hunk.

Old man, your problem seems to be quite normal,
Although I could invent a name more formal.
Your symptoms bother many whom I see.
Who also seem to share your malady.

Turns out the ail that is ubiquitous,
Has now affected nearly all of us,
If not with all the medical complaints,
At least with some societal constraints.

There's not a lot that I can say to you,
Except be vaccinated through and through.
Your funk, I do believe, will go away
When the CDC gives its 'okay.'

I'm happy to report you're not so sick.
No bucket are you just about to kick.
I've checked you through and through, my aging buddy
So your concern won't warrant further study.

But do be sure, before your exit's made
We've scanned insurance cards so I'll get paid.
Gosh thanks. I'll leave with high rapidity,
Assured gout's not a co-morbidity.

What to Plant

We sit in her bare backyard
eating sandwiches
in new red Adirondack chairs,
hers, and another for a guest,
on either side
of a small round table.

She has ripped out all vegetation.
Only mulch remains,
waiting to receive she's not sure what.
Now there's no one to help me decide,
she explains.
He used to love eggplant. I just don't know…

She says she wants to paint
the single window frame
on our side of the garage to match
the ones on the house.
There's still a lot for me to do,
she says.

She sets down her half empty glass of milk,
holds up her wrist, points to it and says,
No one's going to say
It's six o'clock and she's not home.
Where is she?
I could go for a walk, not come back
and nobody would ever know.

Her little black dog curls up on the barren mulch.
We both watch her small belly rising and falling.
I finish the last of my sandwich and say,
Let's talk about what to plant here.

I Hear Ravens

I keep hearing rumors of war,
of the end of our improbable world.
I hear ravens, daily declaiming poetry
they write upon dark branches of time:
my own name implied in every chorus.
How can we say such music is ours,
when the wind sang these verses first?

I want there to be a tomorrow,
please believe me, if you trust nothing else.
But I cannot make this happen alone.
Somewhere between what everyone wants,
and what no one needs,
there is a bench we can sit upon,
watch the real world teach us the way,
share our dreams of the night before,
make them matter more than extinction.

It is said that standing on the shore of Lake Louise,
in the heart of the Canadian Rockies,
and the reflection one sees,
makes more sense than the entire history
of capitalism and its penchant for annihilation.
If this is the true nature of the world,
the geometry of the future is bleak,
a house where death entertains
the lies of angels,
leading into perdition
the rest of us by the nose.

I will go then to the mountains,
Will drink from the source of wonder.
To all I meet,
I will bow to the light they offer,
will carry their helpless fears for them,
that they might walk a time
with an open heart,
even on this grief-filled journey,
before rumors or wars
steal the gift of being
from this sad and broken world.

In the Garden

We sat in the garden,
the three of us,
beneath an umbrella
spread wide,
shielding us from the sun,
the nearest star,
yet so far.

We sat in the garden,
the three of us,
drinking a red wine,
deep and fine,
savoring its warmth
from a season past.

A man and two women
talk philosophy
and the painter's art,
while in the garden
trees bloom, flowers fade,
and a white gardenia
burdens the air
with its sweet scent.

The man recites a poem
from memory,
and the women laugh.
Startled, he drops a line
as the thought is lost
like a yellow leaf
from a fig tree fallen,
his old age revealed
for all to see.

Shudder in the Sunset

an old man was walking down the road …
and I remembered a bird in a cage.
The wise old sage
just strolled by
to squint and blink
a wrinkled eye.

I couldn't remember …
when I felt so sad or so far away.
It seemed the sun was setting …
on the last and final day.

Montenegro

For A.P. and R.R.

The sun rests its tired head
on the mountainous curves
of Montenegro, its bronzed heart
aims arrows of yearning
at the Adriatic Sea.

The dancer of Budva pleads
with the wind to return her sailor
to her side, but her words break
against the rocks while onlookers
throw invisible flowers at her feet.

This local legend about loyal love
stirs something within me,
but it's too much for me to bear.
So, I pluck mementos like low-
hanging fruit at tourist stands.
When my friend says,
"Montenegro doesn't hide its light,"
I see her — The woman who dances
at the seaside with her outstretched
arm reaching toward the expanse.

As I sail away, she calls out to me
over many waters and inspires me
to step out of the shadows
and into a whole-souled life.

Forgiveness

> "Forgiveness is meaningful only when one
> can neither forget nor forgive." — James Hillman

By the time I turned the car around
you had your helmet on.
A fresh flashback of those miles,
the thousands we rode together.
Now, leaving the restaurant alone
in your black motorcycle gear,
long white hair flowing behind you,
proud aging Adonis
ready to mount your steed.

I was in search of you
that late afternoon,
mortally wounded by rejection
and my own insurmountable self-doubt.
Rolling down the window,
as tears streamed down my face,
my eyes met yours, hidden
behind glasses, under the hard shell
you had already donned for protection.

"This was not in the plan."
Did you really say that?
The words hit and slid off the
surface of my reeling mind...
Whose plan? I wondered.
From the mouth of a seriously
committed Buddhist I knew
it could not be God's plan
you were referring to.

I had come for some remnant
of kindness or even pity,
once more begging for crumbs
from a carefully measured heart,
laying myself bare yet again:
a willing victim's final mortification
at the end of a long journey;
after a long sleep, abruptly waking,
birthed by the slap of a merciful death.

How is it life can leave us
stranded so, by the side of the road,
lost, completely lost
and without a plan.
Then the guidance of a broken heart
and angels, seen and unseen,
uncover our path to forgiveness:
where we may finally merge
into one great understanding.

I still have my gear,
those layers of assumed safety
I wore while riding behind you.
It's the kind that breathes
so you do not sweat in the
sweltering heat of the journey.
I keep it on the shelf
to remind me how to let
it all gently flap in the wind.

Coming to Rest in the Dominica Botanic Garden, Roseau

Sit here, let the green light heal.
Words can slice, like the blade
that harvests my blossom and fruit.

Foreign woman, alone, absorbed
in thoughts, jogs along the road.

Warm breeze wafts male words:
hazy sense, violent tone — verbal stones.

Target of taunts, she presses on.
The garden opens its paths to the fugitive.

Under the banana tree, the sky
glows green.

Leaf blades curl down,
raindrops slide

along the midrib,
drip, drip, bleed as from a cut

banana blossom. Sunlight
sifts through the leaves'

fine-spun veins. Relief rises
with the sap to the green

chapel of refuge,
umbrella of overlapping leaves.

No Tenderness

Your word for her was mother, but she was
a polar beach, a barren tropic.
You combed the shore for a caress
given and meant.

　Selfish, lazy—you still hear
her words. They bloom unseasonably, shed seeds
like dandelion heads. You chase them to the edge
of the world, watch them fall off. At night you sing yourself
to nightmare, don't dare write the word: poet. Would she rhyme
it with 'show it'? You have a fountain pen filled with blue ink.

　In the predawn light, before
fear awakens, before the day rains on the page,
you push your hand to the end of the line and the next.

　You have words now.

Spring

Birds chirp and flutter
Frolic with the chicks and calves
Foraging for food

Summer

Summer is more fun
Go fishing camping hiking
Great gifts from the sun

Autumn

Red yellow brown leaves
Fall on the ground in forest
All dried and shriveled

Winter

Cold winter attire
What vegetable has layers?
Must be a cabbage...

How to Prevent the Pull of Gravity

Spread silk over wool, birdwoman says.
Yes. Silk over wool.

Gravity pulls you to the earth, grounds you in this life.
Music. Friends. Wool.
       (Spin, weave, give scarves to love.)

Hear heartbeat in wool. Know pulse. Rhythm of love.

Spread silk over wool.
                    Filter of light extracts essence.

Rainbow silk, prism of rough wool
holds (molds) the warp and the woof.
    films the texture with the silk-screen of light.

Silk, spun out of air.
               Life-stuff, moon-made, the birdwoman
                    spins words out of light:
          (Rapunzel, Rapunzel, spin me a dream.
          How do I know your name, princess of the long
              golden hair, spun out of myth—
          Arachne, Rapunzel, Chandra,)

Hold. Center on silk, spread over wool.
      Gravity, Levity,
                   Right, left.
Center. Balance. Choose your space.
      Fill it with light.
The light holds. The word, light, touches the heart of love.
(with love)
Spread silk. Over wool.

For Adrianne Marcus

How is it that I cannot remember who is living, who is dead?

Reading your poems tonight, I want to write back as I used
to do, to question a word, to marvel at a phrase, to wish, once
again, I had written that. I am tempted to claim your poems
that live in my computer as my own. There they are, magically.
Some finished, perfect. Others only a hint of what they might
have become. If only. If only you had had time to finish them.
If only they had been collected into another book. But here
they are, morning pieces that appeared as soon as I opened my
email. Sometimes just the poem. Sometimes a line like "there is
something wrong with the last stanza." I return to that stanza
again and again. I make suggestions. Make it work. Send it back,
hoping I have gotten it right. But when I read it again, the stanza
remains the same. Unfinished. Your unfinished poems live on,
waiting, waiting.

Hidden Words

I write
I do not know
what I have written
I have written beyond these words
to their shadows
the hieroglyphs that hold
sacred meanings within
I cannot read these dark
marks that still live within
what has emerged
on this thin remnant of
etched stone
there is no translation
for the language
of the heart

Friend

We became friends
meeting for tea
talking for hours

She liked every kind of music
except Chinese wedding flute
which she said was
too nasally

I talked about my mom
who was 94
and owned a Chinese wedding flute
how life without her
was unimaginable
but inevitable

I'd like to meet her
my friend said
so when she does pass
I'll know who you lost

Poet's Cramp

Not exactly a block
But an emotional emergency.
And those damned percussive bells
Ringing in the numbness
More like a concussion than a KO.
First a catch in the lungs
The light headaches thinly pounding out
The consumptive drought.
Then, a mawkish vow of silence.
A simple retreat from the truth.

One foolish month it started up again
During an April thaw.
The ideas dangled like gold trinkets,
But every try was an unruly verse.
The voice rambled on eating its words.
How cruel the muse when with a flurry
It inspired everything everywhere.
Even the textures were chaotic.
Every cross out a genetic disorder
A rogue thought for every erasure.

Later the din ceased with veritable vibes.
No longer devilishly lost in subjunctives.
No longer time to treat my scars.
Poems flowed through with radiance.
Rhythms, rhymes, and iambics
Sweet words tapped together like chimes.
Belated truths became ripened fruit.
Motifs, similes, and metaphors,
Fashioned molds to cast images
The mystical onslaught — a reclaiming of privileges.

Oenophile

I love a dry red wine that lives a long time.
An aged Cabernet Sauvignon
Born in a fat grape tinge of blue.
Every taste a clue for its terroir.

A time when the grapes are punched down
And the cap of seeds, stems, and skins
Are submerged over and again with an incessant break,
Crafted to accentuate a nostalgic swirl.

When stained fingers pull at a cluster of fruit,
Amputating the bunch from the vine
At its laterals and makes the trunk sound.
So gentle the spellbound hands in harvest.

Pour sparingly the bottle of liquid black cherry.
That fine disposition in a thin Bordeaux glass.
Then, the tingling at the tip of the tongue.
Voila! your sweet soul is no longer undone.

The Continuous Lament—An Aubade

Neither of us favors the early dawn
Nor the dawn chorus singing us awake.
The fine stirring, slow turning of
Aging lovers. She insensible to my goings
All these years. Never stopping for a last caress
For fear of stroking to sweet excess.

Love has taught how precious the days.
Weather permitting and with a magic wave
A hand can extinguish a feverish flame.
Yet, we know each other through time.
I know you with my eyes closed
Like a blind man retracing steps composed.

Calculating the paths, we follow separates.
With fine adjustment drift widely apart.
We are never quick to learn how passion binds
Through distance and barriers and ill times.
And when we are abed lamenting our fates
I will enfold you firmly like forever awaits.

Threading My Way Out of the Labyrinth

Ariadne, lend me your thread of hope, like a golden hair,
a waterfall of ideas tumbling from the crown chakra.
For in grief and anger I have lost my way,
constructed my own labyrinth and manned it
with my own bullish Minotaur, shut off from life.
Ariadne, light my way back, for I have gone deep
into the maze of psyche, plumbed its wells and corners.
But I am not to stay here in the cavernous dark,
floating in the mystic lake of salt to prophesy.
Now I need air and light, fresh water and growing things.
Ariadne, hand me now the sword of discernment,
help me slay my daily beast, split it wide open,
so it falls away and out pops a new Self,
tender as a spring leaf, moist
as a Monarch bursting its chrysalis.
May I have done with this tomb and sarcophagus.
May the broth of metamorphosis recompose me.
I wait as my new wings dry in the sun, ready
for the launch, eager for the updraft. No more
Icarus but Daedalus, mature in craft, seasoned
by seasons, turning spiral of life, splendid pirouette.
Ariadne, royal daughter, wise princess,
your faithfulness has saved me
that I may return to you and
enfold you with these wings of distant silk.

Lance's Catch

You told me the story,
when you went fishing in Clear Lake
for the umpteenth time with your father,
the man whose approval you knew
you could never win
yet couldn't stop wanting,
but this time was different
because of the blue LSD tab.
(What were you thinking?)

When you hooked your own thumb —
another nervous bungle under his eye —
and watched the blood well,
your father watched you, puzzled,
not the first time;
you felt wonder, not pain,
empathy with the fish,

and maybe with your father.

In memoriam, Lance Wong, 1953-2022

Susan Dlugach

Candle Speaks

You plucked me from a display,
looked at my bottom,
sniffed me
the way a dog checks out another.
You read the label,
hoping it said soy.
Pero no soy.
Soy wax,
probably paraffin,
a petroleum product.
If you had known,
would you have put me in your cart?
Yeah, my gestation lasted eons,
but you still like me, don't you?
You like my shade, pale sage.
You're fond of shady things ...
dappled sunlight teasing through branches
waving their leafy fingers ...
I heard you sigh
when you caught my scent —
notes of vanilla and amber —
I'm stout and tall.
For a candle, that is.
I'll make a stately figure
when you set me
on that fancy glass dish.
You like me. You really like me.
You'll light my wick, watch my flame,
take in the ambiance I create.
Do you have a lover?
When I burn,
remember this:
I'm not renewable.

Keyboard Memory

I stare at the keyboard
those black and whites
when stroked in proper order
bring joy to the heart
and mind

I remember, I was twelve
fingers found the notes
always in the right place
to produce perfection
every time

Sixty years and more gone by
I sit alone and wonder why
I can't get through Für Elise
even with the pages there
to read.

I know these hands played this once
but now they've lost their memory
and even touch does not remind
of what they once knew
so well.

On the Margins of Nothingness

and even for some generations which she explained to me
thick mix of blue sky where one person begins and another ends
it has Tibetan meaning caseloads of instructions
you could take possession of a person or things with a strong gaze
talk to them straight from the beyond
of qualities you have connected to deep earth longing
her t-shirt was light blue and resplendent with Buddha image
whyever she said
she didn't want a plain metallic piece for her necklace
it would have no more depth than a smoky opacity
I heard her terrors as well as her desires highly polished
whether it translates back to the sacredness of the earth
her hair gathered up in a bun she fingered lovingly
right on I thought drawn to those living on the margins
of nothingness
she had earrings dangling that were colorful to conquer old age
veiled in a longing to be known we chatted
not so bad really her suggestions
the woman with one eye the rings on her fingers and the striking
    lapis lazuli
set in silver
her gaze that could take possession of a life completed

Baking Bread

My favorite bread comes from a Swedish grandmother,
a recipe brought from far-off times and far-off shores.
First track down ingredients and Pyrex pans.
Pitfalls abound: yeast too old? No wheat germ?
Honey turned to cement? Oil smells off?
Gather it all, combine, and create a sponge.
Leave it alone till it doubles in size — just wait.
Wait till the yeast makes the mixed flours breathe.
Wait till the sponge puffs up, high and soft.
Wait till the gluten's elastic and warm.
Then punch it and squeeze it with knuckles and fists.
Slap it around till you're both out of breath.
Once again, wait while it rises.
Wait where it's warm, where it's peaceful and dark.
Wait while the yeast makes the loaves come to life.
Wait while each loaf climbs the sides of the pan
No shortcuts. No skipped steps. Dough takes its time…
Then bake and inhale the aroma of bread:
bread fresh and soft, coming warm from the oven,
warm for the family — *My how you've grown!* —
Welcoming children now busy and bearded.
Sit at the table and savor the bread.

After

After the death and the rites,
absence settles in
like a stranger sharing a bus seat.

Walks alongside the shopping cart
pointing out the brand of beer
you'll never buy again.

Unearths, from the hamper, a sweatshirt
you'll never wash and dry again,
and several unmatched socks.

Puzzles over the Corvette in the garage,
the car he wanted in his teens,
the car no one ever drove.

Unsettles his hissing, spitting cat,
who only puts up with one person,
and loudly protests all those not him.

So give away shoes and clothing,
the old bowling ball,
the aquarium long between tenants.

Keep the guitar, the djembe,
some Miles Davis CD's
Learn to talk to rooms full of silence.

After the death and the rites,
 the familiar flow echoes with ripples
from a life sunk into the heart

like a living stone

Him

His birth family has found him
They hail from Colombia
All 154 of them

He is my beloved son
Raised with love from birth
His birth family has found him

I give him space
To embrace his familia
All 154 of them

I treasure him
Our family of four
His birth family has found him

They treasure his attention
Call him each day
All 154 of them

We are his destiny
They are his birthright
His birth family has found him
All 154 of them

Her

She is an orchid we have watered
fertilized with nourishment and love
Her stem is slim but strong
She knows only one way to grow—
toward open space
grasping reachable air
Her gentle bouquet cascades
along the soft curve of her arm
a tender waterfall of blossoms
She faces the sun
commanding the light to find her
feed her
She presses forward
single-mindedly away from the soil
as if she's waving
a winning lottery ticket
Her petals brush each other
And share a laugh
Her lush leaves find the breeze
and dance their heart out

Snapped

Under the unlit sign
of a 12th street diner
named for an immigrant
dead 20 years now
I lingered
in a fogless twilight
and counted the satellites
in their unwavering arcs
and with each clipped breath
I stripped another layer
from my ill-defined discontent
until
in the unfriendly darkness
I found
with no layers left
you were never to blame.

No Returns

I never thought of you
as the burrito type
but there you sat
on that bench in the park
under the oak tree
tearing at cheap silver foil
with your long black fingernails
while disobedient beans
tumbled away
and you didn't even care
when they landed
on the peach-colored skirt
that came from Saks
because it was funny
what he just said
it must have been funny
because you laughed
a little too bubbly
with just enough jiggle
to make his mouth twitch
before he leaned in
and you welcomed his kiss
and that's when
I turned up Main Street
thinking today I'd get soup
or maybe a salad for lunch
instead of a burrito
and maybe tonight
when turning out the light
at bedtime
I would ask
if you had kept
my receipt
for that skirt

ABC Elegy for Allan

Able and agile
    stepping from rock to rock.

Boulders broken from rock face
    or dropped by glaciers
Caring and thoughtful
    to a fault.

Dying imperceptibly
    then crashing downhill.

Effort increasing to move that hand,
    to read those words.

Forgetting what happened when.
    Mid-sentence hesitation.

Guitars not played and silent.
    Self-written songs not sung.

Hats hanging by the door.
    Hikes halted.

Inspiration for young scientists.
    Your legacy.

Maureen Eppstein

The Price of Vanity

In high school art class once
my teacher praised
a scribbly drawing
of my pinkie finger

She enthused
how sweetly it emerged
from random lines
how well-defined the curve
of flesh and knuckle

Now that stuck-up digit
many decades later
will not join its fellows
in a fist without a fight
nor pull itself upright again
without a click
of bone on bone

Spring Planting

old black plastic six-packs
mix of sand and compost
scooped from plastic bucket
finger-tamped in place

seeds from crumpled packets
feather-light in hand
snow peas for early green
calendula for color

rainbow chard
whose knobby spheres recall
that Buddhist farm
the season's first seed planting

ancient chant in misty air
a smiling crowd
in turn we take a seed of chard
place reverently in a cell

Changed Words Bring Change

it has been written
it has been read

it has been said
change is going to come

seasons change
nature changes

bring change
to the nature in us

change your words
change the world

the change is in the words
what you say changes the world

Mother Teresa said

I will never attend an anti-war rally
when you have a pro-peace rally, invite me

hear the power in the words
seize the power of the words

seize the power
change the world

be positive about change
listen to what is said
hear what is said

words are the seeds
plant peaceful change

be peaceful about change
bring peaceful change

be the change
to bring change

This Stumbling Heart Has Raven Wings

This stumbling heart
softens with rain
rooted in embers
a rambling spring
genuflects in grief

This stumbling heart
grounded in silence
a fallow field
raw with humility
hammock of sorrow

This stumbling heart
alive with astonishment
weeps with kindness
bows in awe
lives within circles of being

This stumbling heart
sheds tears of stone
aches with unknowing
seeks worthiness
is wordless

Last Thoughts

Did I get it right?
Did I give enough love to those who needed it?
Did I put their desires ahead of mine?
Was I strong when I had to be
But compliant when it was better to bend?
Was I forgiving to those who wronged me?
Did I befriend those who were left behind?
Did I rejoice with those who excelled?
Did I give comfort to those who grieved?
Did I get it right?
If not
Will I get another chance?

PaPaw

When PaPaw was young
he looked like Sean Connery
dark hair slicked back and
a smile that said, I'm all that
and whipped cream on top.

A few decades later
he was rail thin, shoulders hunched,
wrist bones sticking out of his cuffs,
no hair to speak of.
We grandkids tiptoed around him.

He teased my little sister when
she found a sparkling black rock,
just sure it was black gold.
He told her, "No, that's a pig turd."
and he laughed and laughed.
She held her ground, mumbling
"NO, it's black gold…."
Then he went to stoke the fire
in the big rusty oil drum where
he burned the trash every day.

He died when I was eleven.
I was sobbing after the funeral.
My mom was touched.
I was just sad that we
missed the school play.
I had a lead role and
the funeral had taken all day.

Glitter

My first reaction was to cover my face
as I felt the prickly glitter
landing there in showers
One-two-three-
and I blinked awake
to see your 3-year-old smile,
chubby glitter-covered fingers
working above me.

"GRRR.... you woke the tickle monster!"
I started crawling after you across
the thick knobby carpet, shaking my head,
shedding colorful glitter from my face.
You ran giggling into the kitchen —
there was shelter between Mommy's soft black leggings
and Truffles' furry wiggling body.

Ohh.... No... the glitter box
is no more.
No more of Truffles bounding to the door.
No more Joni in the kitchen cooking dinner.
No more smiles, wiggles, giggles.
It was just the tapping of
rain
on the roof
that woke me.

The Hollow Stag Dreams

The loneliness in its eyes
Blood flowing over bones
As we watch the red sun dies
Bubbles bursting all alone
Eternity has a longing hand
And footprints last longer in concrete
Than they will in sand
There's no surface tension
Livid is the lilting light
That shines upon the mind
Unkind are the truncheons
That unsightly souls unwind
Disparaged, discarded, disregarded
Blind
Riveted in us rests the divine
Life is a trail. I want to run forever
Though my heart screams
Bleak stormy weather
The hollow stag dreams
A feast before the denizens
Slabs of black venison
Putrid oozing bleak ichor
Runs down the chin of oblivions Vicar
Into the darkness, you tread as that lilting light fades
Lost to the touch of death's warm embrace
From the teat of hope you will soon softly wean
And laid out before you the hollow stag dreams

Eye of the Storm

It's a tornado — the diagnosis
I've only seen ones on T.V. and Toto over the Rainbow.
I sit across the doctor's desk and when he says autism
the room darkens and spins into a grey funnel

I see all my son Owen's records flap away like crows
a grey funnel of assessment scores spin round me in slow motion
words and numbers fall off the page scatter in the wind.

The doctor's mouth moving
but I can't hear the words
only rushing wind in my ears.
Finally I make out the words
"Any questions?" he asks.

This tornado follows me home.
I sit in the eye of the storm
where it is still and quiet.

Owen's baby book   cute pictures toys everything
familiar whirls around and ends up in different places
where I won't be able to find them again.

Act of God? Why did You do it? No answer.
Only silence here at the center where I
watch everything we've ever known fly from us.

Warning siren screams find cover   hide quick
but the siren's coming out of Owen's mouth.
I pull him close out of the storm.
Rock him back and forth.

Morning Tai Chi

Alone in my room,
I practice Tai Chi.

Cloud hands wave to the east.
Fair lady shuttles west.

White crane spreads its wings,
To heaven and earth.

I grasp the bird's tail,
And fly to the mountain.

After My Daughter Moved to L.A.

Her room is bare
except for indigo stars
that dot the ceiling,
a photo of cousins
on a pine shelf.
Useless to her now—
trophies, beanie babies,
soccer ball—
stuffed in boxes
in the garage.
She doesn't know
when she'll be back.

Beyond the window
the limbs of the orange tree
she'd chosen at fifteen
are fruit-heavy,
and I wonder if
the hummingbird nest,
a threaded round dab of gray,
will hold.
But the mother grasps
what's at stake: the two
pale eggs beneath her,
and the beaks, sharp
as fountain pens
that will some day
point to the sky,
undaunted.

Daft Tongue

You mad tongue
translating thoughts
phrases half-thunk
to words
without first consulting
the brain
to be sure of what you're saying
that you've chosen the right phrasing
going off on tangents
making an idiot fool of your owner
but not master
making her regret not rehearsing
so she can guide you   ha
a bit more correctly into the right direction
of her thoughts
not letting you lead the way waggling wildly
with words that did not perhaps
get interpreted the way they were meant to
did not mean what they might have said
what fool this mortal and her tongue can be
not to mention willy-nilly written words
she doesn't know if she's the captain of her ship of fools
or an example other fools can aspire to

1. Windbreaker

Wind whips our wide beach
Drink stinging sand in coffee
No spring waves to ride

2. Stockholm Spring

Soft ice lingers in shadow
The Arctic wind is damp
Wild-eyed kids know it's time to dig

3. Two Toddlers — 2012

The spring of five colds
Plus a burst ear drum and the flu
We watched snow melt through the window

In the Zoom Room

Un-Mute yourself.
Speak up!
Don't hide
behind
a rainbow or a rock,
but look
at everyone:
their eyes, their face —
imagine their embrace.

Feel for the floor.
Acknowledge space.
Take a breath.
Greet all that enter.
Don't sneak snacks.
Leave room for others.
Don't slouch, sit up, straight backs.

Make sure you seem
Intelligent
With books behind you
Or a wall of family photos.
Put on a fancy shirt
Over your pajamas.

Mute yourself!
Don't hog the air
What you tell your dog or husband,
We don't want to hear.

And if you freeze
and get ejected
into that grey
amorphous area
of cyberspace
with no one there
to care

just hold your breath
and let the wheels turn
until you join your friends again
in boxes and in rows
in Zoom repose.

We may never
hold hands again
our bodies languishing
in couch or office chair
having our separate thoughts
craning our necks
to get closer
stuck together
yet alone,
wondering

what is this shrunken fruit
withered on the edges
dried up and neglected
what is this plum pit in my chest
once called my heart.

Age

Age (ing)
Age (ism)
Age (ist)

Age offered as shared identity
—like personal pronouns
intended to be welcoming

—indicating safety
—a safe place to be
—a point in time

Accumulated
like picture frames on mantle.

Keepsakes in curio cabinet—
on display but not intended
to be touched.

Dusted every so often
but otherwise relegated
to memory.

Self-Portrait

I used to be part French horn
and Great Blue Heron.

Mountains in Kentucky
and desert in New Mexico.

I know this because each of these tokens
Have taken a piece of me

—like vapor off dry ice.

I know these parts of me are gone
because I can no longer find them

when I search for them.
Only the negatives of memory remain

—like stains on shirt collars or coffee mug.

The experience leaving its mark
before being consumed,

digested and breathed
back into the air.

Indian Summer

Sneaking in after crisp autumn nights, after leaves have
turned gold, after harvest is done. Sneaking in before
snow starts to fall, before ice coats the pond, before
frost covers trees. Soft, warm days of Indian Summer
tricking us to forget winter is sneaking in. A glossy-
eyed fly crawls inside a stoneware bowl. Red jam calls
him. Crimson and gold leaves ride atop a crystal stream
rushing toward winter.

Breakfast Table

A glossy-eyed fly
crawls inside a stoneware bowl.
Red jam calls him.

Leaves

Crimson and gold leaves
ride atop a crystal stream
rushing toward winter.

The Long Mountain Alive

Pele is the earth-eating woman
Goddess of the Sacred Land
She's eating Mana — Life
As she stirs it now anew

Pele speaks to my treasured things
The Eternity I've ever known
Such I hold in deepest value
She takes with her warm embrace

Pele lives in my deepest dreams
Stirring, slashing — Awakening
Jealous for my lasting love
She burns away all false desire

Pele is born of fertility
Alone she stokes her long canoe
And gives birth to fire!
Then dances hula like lava

Six Rules

Do you have any rules
For spiritual practice?
I do. Let me share them with you.

One—there is nothing to do.
Two—there is nowhere to go.
Three—your native tongue is just fine.

Four—what you're wearing now is great.
Five—there are no other rules.
Except, and most especially, Six—

Whatever you do, wherever you go,
Steer clear of all people and groups
Who strangely start sentences

With these two words:
"May" and "Let."
And that should just about do it.

Rats!

They live in my house and pay no rent.
They eat my food without my consent.
They come and go as they please
Without ever having to sign a lease.

I eat what I eat and I trash the rest
Maybe that's the perk they like best.
My wasteland of leftovers tossed
Bears a hefty rodent control cost.

You can hear their little pitter-patter
And catch bits of their social chatter.
Upon sight, I shriek loud with dread,
I jump onto a chair, my face all red.

Masterful scavengers of ill repute,
They have a sense of taste astute.
That poison you used yesterday?
Identified. They know to stay away.

Three minutes they can hold their breath,
A three day paddle brings them no death,
For up to a mile they can valiantly swim,
They are super fast and also super trim.

Squeezing through a nickel-sized hole
Sharp memory leads them to their goal.
They can disgustingly eat dead flesh
While also devouring everything fresh.

With wild abandon they know to breed
Producing more and more mouths to feed.
And as if that's not enough, they jeer,
Our teeth grow up to 5 inches a year.

Too dignified to pant or to sweat,
Their long tails do temperature set.
Sumatran rats are as big as cats,
Thank God they send us no diplomats.

Most live up to the age of one,
Long enough to destroy just for fun.
They can chew glass and bread
Cinderblock, wire, aluminum and lead.

Impressed as I am with their kind,
It's frustrating to be taken for blind
When it's time for them to make their house,
They line it with my prettiest silk blouse.

As far as I am concerned, reader...listener dear,
Diseases spread by rats invoke much fear,
And although I love Mickey and Jerry a lot,
Ultimately, all real rats deserve to be shot.

The History of the Typewriter

Before touch-screen typing
and quiet keyboards
loud keys clacked and each line dinged
while other predecessors stretched further into time
to styluses in soft clay
and beyond

Choices from the past
echo through to now
sometimes with context nearly lost
like the way "lower-case" letters
were once kept in an actual case
lower down
ready for placement on the printing press
And the way "cliche" was the sound
that those same printing presses made
when repeating a common phrase
over and over again

The location of the keys
on my quiet keyboard
was decided many years ago
by someone concerned with typewriters
and the way those keys could jam
when all struck at once

I would like to talk with that person
discuss their choices
the thought process
and ask if it was truly necessary
to place the "O" and the "I" keys side by side
so that when I go to type "that's worth a shot"
I get something else entirely

Noticing

I've practiced different types of noticing,
the right one at the right time,
to fish for ideas in the shape I need.

The rainbow spray behind a truck tire
while rainclouds amble away
like leisurely rhinos overhead...

That is a poem.

The pratfalls during
a Nerf gun battle with friends...

That's a comic strip.

The typos I make are social media posts;
The idle pondering leads to short stories;
The short stories lead to novels.

But the cat
investigating the toy spaceship
tapping it cautiously with one paw
then springing upward when it beeps
as if she has been freed from gravity by the sound...

Oh, that is several things at once.

Bliss

I paddle farther than intended,
outside the circle of manageable risk.
My surfboard is a fragile ark.
An upsurge could separate us,
casting me beyond sight of shore,
or sweeping me into the hurtful rocks,
unable to climb or swim to safety.

The pungent fragrance of life-rich ocean,
the brisk water and chilled air dancing on my skin,
and the calls of seals and seagulls punctuating time.
I...Am...Intoxicated
without the drag of any drug,
as if the sea were dreaming me into place.

There is still day left
though sunset began an hour ago.
As I wait for the right wave,
the tides shimmer—
bioluminescence
from energized plankton
emitting light
across the moving sea.

Then, I see a giant wave,
white-crested
from glowing plankton and the rising moon.
I feel the insatiability of a dream,
the hunger for a moment
unwrapped from the past.

I pray I have the courage and skills
to stand and ride the wave home,
that the now-bright moon
can guide me to that thin heart of sand,
the golden beach where it all began.

Flowerance

A black baseball cap on a man's head
proclaims NO VIOLENCE in red letters.
His hat flaps in the testy breeze, then flies off,
like a gun bursting
into blossoms of kindness.

Lockdown Nostalgia

I never dreamed
I would long for the heavy, locked, wooden door,
for the isolation that severed me from
friends, cohorts, family, and the wider world.
I never dreamed
I'd long for tiny screen squares lit like candles
to link faces of the known and previously unknown.

I never dreamed
that my wife and I would move from
separate lives occupying disparate geographies
to a maze of walls, passages, house keys, and cups
that guide us to new intimacy;
how my son, who had ignored phone, text, and email,
now called morning and night from his electro-mancave;
how my cat sprawled on the bed with abandon,
in her own way saying, "See what you've been missing?
For the first time, you enjoy the grace of place;"
how Ellen, a goddess of spirit and creation,
appeared online from nowhere, her plant jungle
looming behind to pollinate every conversation;
how I changed from scavenging through market
with a red plastic basket and finding little,
to extolling the miracle of
discovering everything at once online.

As COVID retreats, I implore you,
let us keep the inner door open,
let the messy path of love spiral out
to the golden threads of the universe.
Share with me the hope

that we won't forget our new history.
Pray with me that we stay connected
with Zoom friends and pandemic priests.
And come with me, help me carry
these love diamonds into our physical present.

Reunion

Dad gets out of the car, anoints me
with his gift of a pink hula-hoop.
Again and again, I try to steady
the revolving ring. He smiles,
waits under the old pine.

My son shouts, Mama, look!
His yellow circle takes me back
to that day in July when I,
too twirled and danced inside
my orbit of dreams.

Dad long gone, I glance
at the shimmering sky, wonder
if my boy will return to visit
this summer day. At the center
of a halo, spinning with joy.

Phone Tree

Thank you for calling your friendly Shop & Shop.
Using your touch-tone telephone,
please select from the following choices:

For the bakery, press one.
For sugar highs and lows, fear of gluten, press two.

For the meat department press three.
For clogged arteries and methane gas, press four.

For the produce department press five.
For a list of pesticides and GMOs, press six.

For electronics, press seven.
For binge watching and gaming addiction, press eight.

For the floral department press nine.
For guilt over infidelity and trashing the planet, press ten.

For the pharmacy, press eleven.
For insomnia, worrying we're a bunch of idiots, press twelve.

For all other inquiries, please stay on the line and sob.
Or run to your nearest forest, climb a tree, never leave.

The House Up Little Lake Road

Think about the sun peeking through
a shutter still hanging by its hinge
waiting for wind to send it uphill,
how light pushes outward against
crumbling walls,
how the breeze gently strokes
the overgrown wild mustard
like the touch of a beloved's skin,
and the days roll over
the sagging roof
leaving remnants of memories,
and glitter in the blue, blue everywhere,
sky touching the ground
wrapping its arms around you
and your lungs fill with the stillness
of everything fresh and wide,
and the small knocking of the heart
reminds you
you are the first singing light,
you are the pulse
that keeps this house warm.

Unexpected Spring

I rarely notice the abandoned house,
empty dark-eyed,
forlorn windows and peeling paint.

But today, walking into town
I pause — yellow daffodils —
line the drive,

a chorus of hallelujahs
heads bobbing
in time to the wind.

O heart stirs, you are pulse
and rivulet, a treasure of fire,
transparent angel wings.

You are lift and flight of giggle,
unexpected light that fills in
the winter cracks
I carry under my skin.

Solstice

Sometimes a *grief steps out of the woods*
arriving just as evening begins

I have no words to ward it off
nothing left to wad and throw

nothing left that does not
wake with wound and hunger

only dry stones under my tongue
the same few notes that begin the song

It was the fold of winter
when he died

Prayers in the Shape of Wind

For what else might happiness be
than to be porous, opened, rinsed through
by [the] beings and things? J. Hirshfield

For laughter
that pours out like water
in the music of a child,
for the stream that floats on its back,
and a melody
you can lean into
always here.

For memories
that desperately hang on
like the fledgling's last down,
a whisp of fog twisting
its hair around a tree's fingers,
and those who return from the river
telling us just relax,
what you need will eventually come.

For departure
another candle snuffed out
leaving only a dance
of smoke
riding this thick air,
a startled silence
when crickets pause
to let winter pass

For rust
a scherzo of fire,
a withdrawal
that decays the ploughshare
in its brief triumph,
yellow mustard
growing from its crevices
fragrant and wild.

Meditation on Discomfort

patient as rest's true nature
yet bobbing like an
unmoored lifeboat
searching for the wisdom of water

momentarily suspended
unsure in this tsunami of distortion
sometimes wandering
into the questionable

questions ride the waves
words flow into
a watery thesaurus of language
vision clear only from the crest

pinned by circumstance
power drains to nowhere
deep love embroiled
where it does not belong

Angels of Mercy

they have long carried the promise
they are lighter than air
they have shouldered the heavy
our hopes, our dreams, our recoveries
they do not know the now
they live in the all of wonder
we inform them of our need
they respond with love and clarity
I worry for them
and with shadowed gratefulness
for our own stamina

Last-Minute Gift

Was the cake too big,
Or the pan too small?
Never mind: Frost it

Poets

Give me your song,
Rain Warbler, and I will give you
My umbrella

Stray

Something just ran in
Yellow eyes behind the boots
Now it won't come out
I give it milk, think of names,
How about 'Forgiveness'

Regrets

In the laundry room
There is a wicker basket
Filled with unmatched socks
Each week when I do laundry
I throw another one in

Unpotted

Fallen from a shelf
Thrown out the door — leaves, roots, and
Broken pottery
The dying plant winks at me
As if to say
   Free at last

Sunday Dinners Reconciled

She takes a moment
to remember
the oven door
closing,
squeak then soft thud,
a roast sizzling
inside.
Her father always did the Sunday cooking.
He pampered the gravy,
dark brown drippings
turning tan when he stirred in the milk.
Peas from a can,
potatoes mashed, baked,
sometimes from flakes.
The table set with flowery Melmac
like wheels on a festive cart.

For a man who as a boy was half-starved
the meal was an achievement:
"My children will not go hungry."
For a child who was sensitive to textures
the meal was a gauntlet
of gristle and mush.

As she remembers
the kitchen,
the spoon stirring circles,
the knife cutting through,
she wishes she could say
the thank you
that got stuck

behind the meat she couldn't swallow.
She wants to say,
I understand.
And
the gravy—
that gravy
spread thick on a slice of bread
cut into nine equal squares,
salty, peppery, smooth.
She wants to say
I'm sorry
that was all I wanted.

Filling Voids

The nails should be set deep into the wood,
the resulting hole filled, then sanded level.
A bead of caulk should be run along the edge
to fill any gaps between the wood and wall,
then priming and painting.

That's the way it should be done.
When finished, the molding, trim, and baseboard
should look like they grew out of the wall,
a continuous unbroken surface,
a placid morning sea.

The thing will be stable without these extra steps,
but the pleasure of the eye will be lessened
with holes and nail heads interrupting like reefs.
What does it take, anyway — more bending,
kneeling and stretching, an extra day for drying?

Most of my life I never knew about these skills.
So when my pop renovated the kitchen back in '84,
I thought, how sweet the chair rails and baseboards looked
against the wallpaper with its strawberry vines trailing.
Now I keep noticing the nails and voids.

Didn't he know? Or did he choose to omit the steps?
In all his years of fixing tractors and cars,
maybe he never learned about working with wood.
So unlike him, though,
to be satisfied with less than perfection.

I think about going over his work,
setting the nails, filling the voids.
I'd leave the molding in place,
I'd just fix it, make it right,
smooth it like the brow of a sleeping child.

Faith

You speak of faith like it's a simple thing
but it spears me to my core
and the chasmal wound leaks from my eyes.

I cry over everything these days.

The way the fog hugs the tree line on quiet spring mornings.
The moment my aloof cat decides my fetal position is her resting
    spot.
The thought of my husband's side of the bed remaining
    untouched
Or the day my last child leaves home for good.

But mostly, I cry over the faith I left behind,
over those I wish to forget,
and for those who forgot me
a bit too easily.

It will always be the ornate stained glass,
the musky smell of incense,
the resonant sound of the choir emulating seraphim in the rafters.

It will always be the well wishes,
the sense of belonging,
the intertwining of our lives through shared beliefs.

What once was Maundy Thursday
is now Black Saturday,
when the world sits in a shadow.

I will always be here in the waiting.

And my spirit, once tethered,
now wanders this variable land,
searching for something to cling to,
missing that whisper of time
when everything made sense.

Now that I've tasted the pomegranate, I can never go back.

And yet, here I am,
listening to your faith.
For a moment I'm jealous that you stand where I stood.
That you don't know what I know.

My tears both cleanse and drown me,
washing my wounds with their stinging salt.
And I hastily brush them aside,
hoping you won't notice.

How do you not notice?

Yet, you keep talking,
even as the current between us grows.
But your hand rests on my arm,
and I picture God herself,
letting me know my tears belong
and so do I.

Thighs

You don't know me
And I don't know you
But while the speaker drones on
Our thighs have become intimate

Perhaps they are filling time
As they spill onto each other
The fabric of our pants
Their only barrier

I had thought I would be bothered
By their shameless affections
Wondering when they'd notice
They were drawing attention

But in this cold, crowded room
Your thigh brings me comfort
And I teeter without balance
when you stand for the ovation

Yet when you return
Your thigh nuzzles mine
Continuing the affair
While we remain strangers

"Who Are You?"

I watched, a silent observer waiting for a flicker of familiarity to return.

"I am your wife," said she with a tone like a familiar song hoping the waves would penetrate the foggy memories of her husband of twenty-eight years.

"You're not my wife," he barked.

"Yes, I am, don't you remember when we danced beneath the harvest moon…"A lighter shade of pale" blasting across the meadow? Annie, and Phillip and Steve, plus your kids and mine showering us with pink rose petals? Remember?"

He eyed the white sock slipping off his right foot shaking his head. Bending, he fumbled to tighten loose laces of the weathered boot upon the other foot.

"My wife got me these boots," he declared. "At the Army surplus store—Where's my flight jacket? It's time to fly! I could still take off from that flight deck, you know. It's like riding a bike or sex…"

"And after the wedding," said she, not missing a beat, "we honeymooned in Mendocino while watching for whales and sipping coffee…smelling the salty sea…"

"I loved that smell especially returning from a mission at dawn…" he trailed off, again.

She bent at her narrow waist, voluptuous cleavage heaving beneath her summer top, and kissed him, soft lips upon his stubbled cheek.

He leaned back, head tilted, with a smirk, "Hey, I know you. You're my wife!"

"And I always will be, 'til death do us part."

"Have you seen my keys? I want to go for a drive…"

How Much Indian Are You

a stone's throw across the river
twenty feathers off the hawk
one fry bread worth
twenty flute songs
a bundle of tobacco
a pint of blood pumped
from my mother's heart
according to the chart
the doctor missionary
author anthropologist
will tell us our ratio
if we are authentic or not
who is telling our story
a distant relative sold
land traded for frog skins
with a small forest of trees
to close the deal
an auntie ran off with
a French fur trapper
they moved to town
bringing us forward
then down
cohabitation regulation
assimilation eradication
papers needed to cross
a line
however you measure
I'm keeping my treasure

Among the Wild

It's a wonder to catch a glimpse
of the animal wild within
that hasn't been punished out of us.

To yawn like a cat, lick a plate clean
to hear an ancient primordial scream
of a soon-to-be mother.

To receive a love-bite short of blood,
to roll down a hill with your cubs.
Morning yoga, downward-facing dog,

a sun salutation.
Pulling socks up in the morning
taking them off at night.

You slide open the back screen door
walk out to the crickets and evergreens
give out a howl under a crescent moon.

When final rest comes
you'll lie down with the lichen, toads,
night crawlers; fastidious ants.

Smell the mushrooms in midnight grass,
aaaah. And then you'll remember,
remember—

the wild in you.

Pietà

Leaned back;
soft supple branches
hold up the tree that has
fallen into it
    day in and
    day out

under a full moon
by the waterfall
branches meshed together

like a nest.

Here We Don't Say Alzheimer's

Mangos and avocados
lined up on the window sill
a fresh plucked tomato in winter.

Dishes all dried and put away
plants watered, counters wiped off
and there's always fresh coffee.

My friend smiles at me innocently
as if I were in on the secret.

Oh

to glide like a leaf, said the bird

to be light as a feather, said the leaf

to be free as the wind, said the feather

to have form, said the wind

Speak From the Heart

Anything essential that yearns to be expressed emanates best through the heart. Far too frequently, contrivances become taxonomized purely from the head. Allow wisdom of the cardiac organ to suffuse emotional elements that hold expanse for concepts to be digested. Not just through thought, words, but space and energy. Facilitate greater elucidation. If I say to you, look at the difference in the shades of green on this tree compared to that. You notice a distinction. If I instead point out that shorter days unmask and display the leaf's diverse, underlying chemical colors. Consider such a contrast. When hearts protect, comments roil the atmosphere.

Every Day

Someone dies, someone
you knew, someone from school, from work,
from down the block, from that time
you lived in the hippie town on the coast.
That guy who gave you the last little bit
of cocaine you ever had in 1983

Your ex, your not quite ex, your
wish-he-had-been an ex,
your best friend, your good friend
The one you secretly lusted after,
the one you not so secretly lusted after.

The poet, the singer,
the neighbor with the barking dogs,
the nice neighbor who baked bread
and brought you loaves
all through the pandemic,
loaves you still can smell
every day when you open
your otherwise empty
great-grandmother's
faded metal
breadbox.

Full Moon in Cancer

While watching for the green flash of sun dipping into ocean, I see instead
Lost Island of Atlantis   rising from the sea
   obscured by fog or rain or industrial haze This vision
          must unfold every evening
          about this time

Clouds shrouding majestic columns backlit
    by otherworldy radiance
    are nothing less than mountains where gods live,

drinking their nectar, getting rowdy with each other and, sometimes,
    with us   poor mortals hoping only for an atmospheric trick of light
      and the
    rising of the full moon in Cancer
    in Bolinas California.

The mirror opens again.

A Kind of Silence

it wasn't exactly quiet
music drifted over
from the picnic area
acorn woodpeckers
called raucously from the oaks
a rooster crowed somewhere
across the river

it was more a kind of silence
such a silence that comes after
a great speech
in the moments after it ends
when the speaker's wisdom
floats in the air

like the wisdom of the river
and the trees
the river flowing in front of me
deep and still
the trees surrounding me
with presence

Tip Up

The big oak
lay on the forest floor
roots dangling in air
branches flattened
to earth
I wondered
Did she sense it coming

I observed the sandy soil
hardpan beneath it
surmised her canopy
was just too heavy
for shallow roots
and then there was the rot
starting in her center

it must have been the
big storm last night
blowing in from the west
who knew it would be the one

other trees came with her
pulled down or crushed
it really wasn't their
time to go, or was it

who knows what is written
in the stars
how we are all connected
how the sunlight pouring in
will give rise to new life

how one tree falling
can be another tree's rising

I Do Not Travel Far in August

when squash
unfurl stars
in my garden

when tomatoes
come out of hiding
ornamenting
pole beans
and peppers

when zinnias
parade
on long stems
each flower
proclaiming
summer
will not end

when maidenhair
mounds
in the cool moist
corner
and the shiny
black skink
peeps out

when each gaze
fills me
completely

I do not
travel
far
in August

Wild Heart

I lie down on the ground
feel the soft litter
of leaves and twigs
moist soil and fibrous roots

sink deeper
into lower strata
onto rock
continents and oceans
floating upon it
drifting together or apart
mantle and crust
the shell of the earth

I close my eyes
sink deeper still
imagine earth's fiery core
primordial, dense
pulling me inward
body to ground
ground to core
wild heart
to wild heart

Star Chatter

when earth's face
turns away from the sun
and in the darkness
we can see the stars shining
listen
for they are talking too

find a dark silent place
lie down under a sky
full of stars
feel them draw close
cover you with a blanket
of the softest bird down
then listen again
for the star chatter

their various observations
wars, acts of kindness
exquisite beauty, terrible grief
what they make of our travails
what they hope we will do
or not do to save ourselves

Marianne Lonsdale

First Mornings During a Pandemic

The dog tugs me up the sloped cement
In the early morning darkness
Moonlight still shines
On the cracked asphalt street
He lifts his leg and I praise
A gauzy full moon
Rests above and beyond my roof
Over the estuary I cannot see
But know is there
Everything is still here

Rainwater rolls down the muddied ditch
Into the storm drain
Droplets refresh my face
I close my eyes and
Breathe
Interrupted by the garbage truck
And the moon has left
I didn't know she'd be gone so soon

I pull two lemons from my neighbor's tree
Glance up, above the magnolias
Nearly crying out for one more
Glimpse of moon
Before heading home
Everything is still here

The Ninth of April

Nothing happens
On the ninth of April
Except hugs when we pass in the kitchen
And the cool air bussing my face
As I walk my beloved pup
Quiet peace stretched from yoga holds
Finishing that book I didn't want to end
My husband downstairs practicing
Singing while strumming
Letting chocolate melt in my mouth

I learn to wait
I learn to desire
The nothing that happens

This Journey to Ixtlan

They say it never happened,
this journey to Ixtlan.
That this knowledge of ancient peoples
existed only in Carlos Castañeda's mind.
That my whole belief system —
wisdom of the unknown,
this opening to the wonders of the world,
places beyond what I can conceive
and want to touch —
they say he made it all up.

They say that Indian natives
don't have this culture,
that you can't "stop the world,"
that knowing the difference between
hunter, warrior and sorcerer
doesn't lead to a life of knowledge.

But all my spiritual growth began here,
when Paul gave me this book
and worlds opened up.
For others it was Herman Hesse,
for me it was the teachings of Don Juan.

And while drugs and
going back to the land
didn't have the same resonance,
I knew sacred wisdom was out there
for me to discover
at some point in my life —
the ways of indigenous people,

the life that cannot be
logically explained.

They say what he taught
isn't true
but something inside me
knows that it is.

Your Parting

I remember
playing marbles in the hallway.
And Superman—
your jumping off the dresser
onto our bed
to save Lois Lane.

I remember your coming home
with new music,
sharing your excitement of
Dylan, the Beatles, the Doors.

I remember
practicing smoking pot
with oregano in your pipe
so I would know what to do.

All this you handed to me now,
with countless more,
filling me, as it once filled us.

I stand with memories
that will someday be put to rest.
But for now
I accept the gift of this burden,
the carrying forth of the two of us—
alone,
without you.

No Answers

Why did you break it off?
I was drunk on life.
It was the times.

Did you ever love me?
As much as I could.
I was fickle.

But why wasn't I enough?
Greener pastures
If not as sweet.

Did I know the others?
A few from my past,
and the future

Might we have worked it out?
I loved you, but still,
I wasn't ready

What did you want from me?
You were a rare wine.
A sip, a taste

Yet, you drank deeply?
We drank and had fun.
Lost in the dark

And wrong for each other?
Not right, but still close.
Forever friends

Tapestry

The threads of a life
Fabric made from blood and flesh
Sinew and tendons
Weft-faced weaving, tie the warp
Loom of cartilage and bone

Woven together
The pattern tells the story
Life's a tapestry

Backsliding

The secondhand coat I wore in school
no longer fits.
Nor the secondhand ideas.

I miss our high held heads.
Our passed out forms.
All the old forked roads.

I have an urge
for an urge
to smoke.

He's My Brother

In our backyard
behind the one-car garage
we hide in a blackberry thicket.

In this dream sprinklers spray
cold water between our fingers
spider webs catch our hair.

This dream returns you from the dead.
You are wearing torn jeans.
"Tell me about your life."

On the ground fruit rots
covered with flies, apricots
sweet, with brown pits to chew.

Piles of yard rubbish.
A place to hide. We see the sun
dry morning frost.

Out back free, without faces.

I Am Zinfandel Velvet

blood red of autumn orange
entombed in glass
a world inside a world
shapeshifter
voluptuous in crystal
hips aswirl like a dervish
I devoutly meander
trickle and tease
when I squint back to summer vine
my skin still on
I hear coyotes' bantering echo
smell sidewinders
rustle in vibrant mustard
remember wild dance
with mischievous wind

I am ancient habitat of metaphors
nocturnal part of mind
a circle of voices cast
a menagerie to describe me
some say I whisper pepper
exude bristly blackberries
when I meet thirsty tongues
they cock an eyebrow and say
ciao
another splash
bravo

I am a baroque fugue
play a language of
ruby stained glass

abandon earthen bouquet
slithering pomegranate seeds
a relationship forms from
repetitive slurps and sips
boundaries blur
a jingle of midnight
they dawdle then unravel home
invincible
fragile
I am marrow memory
remnants moored
in lonely bottom of kissed goblet

Creativity

"She's a little on the
creative side"
said of me growing up.
Meaning what?
Just because I did things
Like
Stack my smaller dresser
atop my larger one
upside down
their four legs
sticking up like
turkey drumsticks
into the air —

It worked,
saved space in my bedroom
where I stacked books on my nightstand table
next to my bed,
hardly ever read
but thinking the words would migrate
into my head as I slept
and god damned if I didn't get an A
on my physics exam —

So label me a bit weird
It's okay
Didn't Nietzsche say
"Those dancing are called crazy
by those who just don't hear the music."

Kathleen McCarroll Moore

Catching Air

Our guest was a circus performer
a fact that held my grandsons in thrall
spellbound in the living room
wishing for a trapeze to appear
above the fireplace

he regaled them with stories
of diving without a net
and balancing babies
in his open palm

they want to fly, my grandsons

It's time that flies, I tell them
but they don't believe
that once I was as young as they are now
How I stood tall, balanced in the hands of my father
as he lay stretched out on the living room floor
raising me slowly above his head
my arms spread wide like wings

The Unlikely Hiker, Hope Valley, California

I count every step I take
To keep myself going.
I will my pounds forward and upward
To negotiate passage through these woods
Safely and soundly,
To explore both its limits and mine.

Look, I know I'm fat.
I see you sizing up my girth
As if to say, "Oh, honey—
You're not going to make it…"
Not up this incline, not down that descent.
You will never reach that alpine lake
All the guidebooks call divine,
A moderate hike from the trail head,
Doable in a day.

As if a destination is
The only possible, plausible goal
For following a path
Instead of pure motion
And a pulse-pounding journey.
I am clearly not here
For the overland speed record.
I yield right of way
To those on a mission.
I enjoy friendly greetings they toss
Over their shoulders as they pass
And march onward
Toward their Nirvana.

But because I touch the earth more heavily
And move at a slow, aching pace
I experience nature intimately.
I inhabit the places I stop and stand,
Where I rest my knees and hips,
Where I restore my breath and narrow my gaze.

I am here for the crisp conifers—
The prickly Ponderosa
And the gentle Jeffrey—
For the quaking aspens,
Their silvery limbs rattling gold leaves
Like coins in some fortunate pocket.

I am here for the birdsong and insect buzz
Reminding me I am not alone in this world,
That I am just a visitor in their home.
I am here for the granite erratics
The boulders strewn across the landscape
By bygone glaciers,
Reminders of a time past and powerful
A force that, like me,
Moves at a slow, measured pace.

Manzanita

Who carved you manzanita?
your slender mahogany hues
your trunk twisting, arching, curving
delicate arm tendrils
crowned in pale green
light and shadow dance
on your lovely burgundy skin
inviting me to stop, linger, touch
to run my fingers across
the smoothest surface
run my cheek across
a cool hard limb

Your dense flesh
lies close to the ground
in possession of earth-water-sunlight.

I walk along a lakeside trail
early morning mist on the lake
the dread of my human affairs

I run my hands over your spiraling knots
and pray — Dear Mother,
don't let your son
forget your beauty, ever.

Dark Times

Hope crawls on all fours across the carpet
And nestles by your right foot
While you gaze off in the distance,
Disaster movies playing in your heart.
Hope nestles inside your pillow
And injects your fear-filled dreams
With impossible solutions.
Hope refuses to die, or go away for long.
It reappears like the ring around your tub
Grubby and persistent;
Like a buzzing mosquito when you're sure the screen was closed;
That insistent whine, so near, yet invisible.

Drought

Sear earth, shiny with the memory of water
First welcomes the rain like an old, well-regarded lover
With a warm embrace, eyes fully closed, taking in the scent so
    familiar.
Then earth, feeling the weight of so much water,
Spurns further offerings,
Forming runnels, rivulets, courses, a flood.
No one has ever been kind to you she said
And a flood of memories confirmed the fact.
But like parched earth, I said
Enough, enough,
I can't hold any more
After living with so little for so long.

An Old Cowboy Goes to Yoga

Long before I knew him
this midwestern rebel
drank and
smoked and
played his way across the country
along the way
he was a
husband
father
airman
honky tonkin'
rodeo cowboy
with inquiring mind
and a Peter Pan soul.

He ran himself ragged:
broken bones
torn heart
crushed lungs
and ever giving till
depleted

still, the mind
expanding
reaching
teaching

I met his shell
and knew at once
I would have loved
him fiercely in the past

we would have danced the nights away
and likely would have
broken hearts: mine, his as well

Why yoga, why now?
On his way downhill
something made him
change his mind, decide
to live some better time
whatever's left
to stretch
to breathe
to be

I too am breaking down

So now what's left for us
is friendship:
deep, wide, easy
When we hug goodbye
the strength
still in his hands
gives me a thrill
reminds me
how I wish
I'd been his
someone

I treasure what we
have and miss the
past we never shared.

Department of Defense

There is no war,
It's just defense.
There is no loss,
It's just expense.

There are no names,
There's just a list—
No one is lost,
He's among the missed.

They are ignored,
But there's no shame.
They may be punished,
But without blame.

In public view,
All's noble act.
Each looks away,
From actual fact.

When we defend,
What do we do?
It's you hurt me,
And I hurt you.

There's no disdain,
It's just defense.
Like China's wall—
It makes no sense.

On the Serengeti

I feared him before I smelled him.
I smelled him before I heard him.
I heard him before I saw him.
I heard the rustle on the land.
I turned to look and there he was.
      Hungry for fresh meat.

I saw his muscles tense and knew he would make his move.
He ran and as his speed picked up
I cried out to the herd,
"Run! Run! Mothers! Fathers! Protect your children! Run! The lion
   is hungry."

As the protector of this herd, I knew we could outrun him.
  Most of us.

We ran as the spirits guided us. We ran for our survival.

Then I heard it.
The screech of a young one.
The screech of the one who could not outrun.

I knew the lion's want for fresh meat had been savagely satisfied.

We slowed.
  We stopped.
    We bedded down near still water.
    We slumbered.

I walked our perimeter and bowed to the
mother and the father for the loss of their calf.
They cried in the night.

I rested and thought someday that will be me.
Someday I will no longer be the strongest, the fastest, the most
    alert and agile.

Someday I will be running from the hungry lion
as fast and hard as I can, but not fast nor hard enough.

I will be the one the young lion will take down.
   I will satisfy its lust for fresh meat.
      I will be the one sacrificed for the sake of the herd.

I will be the one they will cry for in the night.

Yosemite

As I drive into Yosemite Park,
My shoulders relax. Surrounded by trees.
No flashing lights or noisy traffic,
My breathing slows.

Walking on a path through the Valley,
The quiet is seductive.
The quiet that brings me back
To this beautiful place.

The quiet that allows me
To hear the birds singing.
The leaves rustling in the wind,
Children laughing in the distance.

Walking to Yosemite Falls,
I hear the falls long before I see them.
A steady pounding of water
On the granite boulders below.

Nearby, a majestic mountain, Half Dome,
Overlooks the valley
The beauty of its granite face,
Draws me in. Mesmerizing.

El Capitan, Sentinel Rock and Glacial Point
All overlook the Valley.
The strength of the mountains
Feels protective, like a bodyguard.

Surrounded by the valley's beauty:
Rivers, pastures, mountain trails.
The mountains holding up the blue sky.

Another world, separated from the city
By the majestic granite peaks.
Quiet that a person needs,
To survive back in the city.

A sublime experience.
So much beauty
Brings serenity into my life.
Its memory will heal my soul.

A Liquid Collage

A mighty atmospheric river,
        an airborne Big Muddy,
has redrawn the landscape
        and made of the ocean
a liquid collage of gray strips
        torn from storm clouds.
In the foreground,
        a wide brown incursion
        carried by the river
        is bearded with foam.
A thin strip of blue clings to the horizon.

On the beach,
        stripped to round boulders,
the rushing water, capricious sculptor,
        has left behind
        a sharply chiseled wedge of sand.

Feathers tousled by the wind,
        heads tucked in,
        a clutch of white birds
        nestles near the surf,
        puff pastries on a sand shelf
        all facing the same way.

Weathered sea stacks,
        seasoned veterans,
        hold position.
Some sport an ice plant beret.

Dances With Bees

She skips outside and gossips with the breeze
Her garden always grows in disarray
She paints herself in stripes to dance with bees

From roots to crown, she'll branch with redwood trees
You may not understand, but it's her way
She skips outside and gossips with the breeze

Her flowers relish time with her, and tease
With sweet and fruity colors they display
She paints herself in stripes to dance with bees

In sun or clouds — or rain or sleet — at ease
She hums along, views lightning as ballet
She skips outside and gossips with the breeze

Banana slugs will bring her to her knees
What conversation happens, she won't say
She paints herself in stripes to dance with bees

She frequents woods, absorbs their harmonies
That soothe, that smooth the edges of the day
She skips outside and gossips with the breeze
And paints herself in stripes to dance with bees

Summer Nights

Uncle Lu's family built a new house,
With a smooth flat stone rooftop.
On summer days,
They spread out grains of rice,
Fresh from the fields,
To dry on bamboo mats.
At night,
After the rice went to sleep in their bins,
As fireflies lit their lanterns and searched for their beds,
We poured water over the roof to cool it,
Swept it clean,
Rolled out bamboo mats for humans,
Lay down to converse with the sky,
Vast and endless,
Reachable with stretched fingers.

Breeze, the playful guest,
Tousled our hair, fluttered our shirts.
Adults talked of land reforms,
Someone's betrothal, a cousin's new job.
We the young debated
Which teacher was the nicest,
Why a man in a movie was so stupid,
Whether the blood on his face was real.
We compared the fish we caught,
The rabbits we fed,
The pink deer-shaped sesame cake we ate.

All the while, the smell of new rice drifted into our noses.
The stars gazed into our eyes.
Our voices diminished,
Soon murmured into silence.
We drifted into dreams,
While the fireflies fluttered on.

Inception

My bones,
pearl white and brand new
grew like tendrils of roots
before the earth of flesh enfolded them
They gleamed in the moon
drank the light into their marrow
refined the nectar of my spine
the clear intoxication ran into my veins and
began singing the rhythm of my heart
the tides of my pulse
I unfolded from seeds and roots until
my imagination enfolded the cosmos
my voice was song and whispered
stories by firelight
My body was dance and thunder
earthquake and supernova

The stars are in my eyes,
in my blood and
in the blood red beet
I pulled from the earth with my bare hands
that grew from the seed
I whispered to before I planted it

The time that passed between seed and harvest
was filled with dreams and trembling
birds migrating like black stars
against the bone white sky
bees hungry in the cold
the footfall of night creatures
breathing out tiny clouds
in the darkness

The heaviness in my body is
the weight of the sun and gravity
multiplied by time
It is the memories I carry
on my shoulders
guarded and locked
for fear that any should escape
Still, they seep out through the keyhole and
mutter in my ear

The Fig

Aphrodite exclaimed as she opened the plump fig,
"Oh, that I could be a tiny seed nestled within,
Or the lingering honeyed taste on the tongue,
Or gaze longingly at the flesh of the fruit,
All glistening and pink."

Buddha sat under the shade of the Bodhi Tree
To discover what would emerge if he stilled his mind
Through his unwavering will,
Through persistent meditative quiet.
With the rough fig bark at his back,
He lost all sense of time.

Adam and Eve roamed their paradise
Clad in the colossal fig leaves
Exposing their modesty
When before there was unashamed innocence.

My young legs climb the ladder.
When tall, lean grandfather steadies the rungs,
Trust fills my heart,
As I reach for the dazzling top,
Searching and reaching as if grasping life,
So new and unchartered.

The orange rays of the sun dazzle me
As I reach blindly for the fruit of my desire.
Confidence fills my tiny being,
For I know I will grasp the sweet essence
If only I stretch my chubby fingers
Toward the timeless clear blue sky.

With his pocket-knife, my grandfather splits the purple skin.
I view the fleshy velvet flowers within,
And savor the textured wonder in my mouth,
Chewing gently and with awe for this miracle.

White Morning

The quiet, white, early morning sky
Envelops me in a cocoon of calm

My double-pane windows mute city noise

I watch birds fly in the whiteness
nothing is torn
no sound is made
no ripple of color

I am peaceful

A meditation
Becomes a vision of
sunshine melting the fog
trees sweeping clouds into view

I rise from my chair
Sliding open the windows
my cocoon splits

I hear
children exclaiming
birds conversing
dogs barking

and

I bow to this new day

On Watch at Sea

I sail on New Passage under a night bright with shimmering starlight.
Silver-green wavelets splash and spray around its white hull.
Alone in the cockpit, as far out as I can see, I keep watch.
Two dings call out on the nautical clock: the nighttime crawl is about
    to lift.
Darkness departs, and my favorite hour arrives at morning's first light.
As the gray dawn touches the ocean's emerald horizon,
I turn all the way around to gather in the earth that surrounds me.
When a sliver of orange sun peeks over the ocean's rim, time's pace
    picks up.
And I begin a new day again.

And Yes — There Are Roses

Love is not a straight shot.
Chronologically speaking, you fall into it a stupid number of times.
Is pain beauty?
Is it what we call that thing that forces us to feel, expand, learn
    empathy?
The journey is loaded down.
Sometimes catastrophically, adult life starts with a jolt.
It's such a shock when the plan doesn't work, the GPS goes haywire.
And suck enters your vocabulary.
A poet wrote: *when we become what we came here to know*
I want to be inside that song, that wisdom.
My mother left me when I was two.
Is this my quiddity — my "whatness?"
Our minds are these wild things that sit atop our physicality and
demand constant mining.
A poet wrote: *There should have been roses....*
Across the waving grass, the sensual flowers, the aroma of
    spaghetti,
It comes to me — life.

Exact Right Life

A strangeness stalks me   the first time
in forever, I think a   something
dropped into the   dark
maybe even into Plato's cave,
or perhaps   into my own
mind
I believe there is   more
I want the corners of my life   to turn
pink   as I go to the
                    sunset
I want my dyed blonde hair   not
to fall out   before
I make it to   the end
Somewhere between tears and coffee,
I need to find
the   exact life
To fly toward the
sun,
to hell with   waxed wings
Let the cup spill,   the juice stain,
I want
to drown in   endorphins
I need to see myself,
to know
these last years   are right
Taste the morning blue of   the sky,
        love my   one life.
Oh
and did I say   I'm
    coming   back

In This Bend of Time

from its perch the yellow bird
summons dawn note by note
like a T'ang lute player

day-blind stars
fade from the window
morning arrives thin as worn fabric

in soft lit air
your breath sounds like
the whisper of sea in a shell

mist moves in willows like smoke,
across the valley there is a suggestion
of rain in low blue-bellied clouds

the world with its ruptures and raptures
its dissolutions and resolutions
calls me into this moment

alive for now
in this curve of time
no longer edgewise to earth

your thigh
beneath my palm
warm as hot sand

in all possible
multiverses
this is the iteration I love:

you curled beside me
casting a spell of home

In Sunlight and Shadow

satin shine of curtains
drape bright and dark
grey shadows curl in cream fabric

sheen of polish
on carved satinwood stools
with grain like golden tides receding

pools of sunlight pinpoint small
intricacies in an Indian carpet
hand-knotted of blue and amber silk

the skull of her face
in a black and white drawing
holds a sharp gleam
like thin bones of angels

our lives are framed
by birth and death
what will the next
resurrection bring us

as we move like reflections
through time
out of the room of objects
into the white wind of eternity

The Extremely Important Works of My Small Life

My goldfish is entirely dependent on me.
I clean its bowl and show up with food every day.
I am God to this fish.
I also vacuum my floors, there is no excuse for detritus.
Regarding the furniture, there is pillow fluffing and dusting.
It all turns to dust.
I talk to the dog, most people do not recognize that dogs are
    interested in politics.
I am always available to open doors for the cat. Sometimes it just
    wants to see me do this
and does not exit or enter.
I keep myself clean. The less said about this the better.
I never answer anything with a 800 or 888 number. Sometimes I
    do not answer numbers
I know well.
I walk to the mailbox. There is so much to recycle.
The plants like their leaves sprayed with a fine mist, not too cold
    or too warm.
I must feed myself. Sometimes I don't.
I remember my mother.
I remember my father.
I remember my friends.
I keep myself busy with my extremely important works.

Shanti Rosenblatt Nears Enlightenment

I wanted to be self-realized by Wednesday. In yoga class I sat in
a semi-lotus position (well ok... I was sitting on the floor). I am
doing well on not being judgmental even though I am surrounded
by feral yoginis. I was well on the way to fulfilling the paramita on
generosity. In meditation I had to stop from congratulating myself
for giving away the contents of my head (this made me mindless...
truth be told I had a running start). I am proud of my flourishing
egoless state. I am also, having spectacular success with my loving
kindness practice. Just yesterday in Nordstrom's, I saw those cute
Prada sandals that would look just right with my Aum sports bra
top and lavender Lululemon stretch capris. I was lovingly kind
enough to purchase them for myself. However, I must admit I am
having a titch of trouble with attachment. How could I possibly
leave those shoes in the yoga studio changing room with that
sign that said stealing is bad karma? Well... that is something to
meditate on and still be on schedule, after all it is only Monday.

Visiting Author

We put her in a jar
and tap on the glass—
How do you get your ideas?
What is your reading life like?
Notepads poised, observing diligently,
watching the merest flutter to determine pattern and behavior.
What is your editing process like?
How do you know when a work is finished?
We dissect her with eager hope.

She is the first specimen to fall into our grasp:
A creature submits to the microscope
and we gingerly prod its protected parts
in the name of artistic knowledge.
When during the day do you write?
How did you find your agent?
At last she is released, back to the
nebulous creative wild from whence she came,
leaving a glow of inspiration that will last
until we catch the next one.

Eye Contact (Autism)

I didn't notice them
but see now
your pupils,
irises dart
stopping
across my
forehead, the steep
of my cheekbones
pausing,

Flame flash behind
your eyes, soaking
in the thoughts behind mine—

Then lifting,
leaving, like the shadowed
glimmer of stars, just
missing
in orbit.

WTC

"Science gives us metaphors for poetry:"
— John Keats

He falls headfirst from the mighty tower,
His arms by his side, his eyes open,
Like one of Galileo's spheres. His life
Is consumed by the gravity of the moment,
At thirty-two feet per second.

He would like to tell his daughter
That the Italian was entirely correct:
Two objects will fall at the same speed
Regardless of the weight of the soul.

Father and Son

The home movie shows you
As you were in 1950:
Undershirt, clodhoppers,
Your khakis slung low.
You fought the good fight
Tending the bare yard
Of that tract house in Tracy.
Three of five children
Tangled between your legs
As you pumped the shovel
In the Central Valley loam.
That summer I was almost two.
My memory has nothing now
But that scratchy celluloid
And the aching, distant sensation
Of the heavy valley heat.

The cassette snaps into place
And I see myself on TV:
I extend my arms and balance
The child; each foot placed
Tentatively, he makes his way
Staggering among toys.
I pick him up and hold him,
Arms wrapped like smoke
Around a burning fire.
He pushes away and strikes me,
Unwilling to be obscured.

In the mirror this morning,
What is this shock of recognition?

I think of the child and then
I see your smile dance across
My lips. Strange double-take:
Your arm around me around the boy.
I feel your ready tears well up:
For me, for you, for the child
Whose pulsing movement
Slaps upon my face
The smile you wore for me.

These Things Are Real

These things are real:
The grip of a newborn's finger,
Fierce in anticipation of a life;
The cry of a child discovering
An insect's iridescent carapace;
The shock of biology,
The punch of first love;
The urgent need and release
Of honest desire;
A hand placed lightly on
A lover's belly as she sleeps;
The balm of your words
Soothing a person's heart;
Three notes played together,
The first, the third, the fifth;
The smell of cut wood
As your hand guides the saw;
The passage of time that teaches
Time is merely an illusion;
That moment when life ceases
And the soul breathes out.

Nothing can change these things:
Not the myth of money, or
The cacophony of want,
The momentary power of status,
The fawning of sycophants, or
The rejection of people
Who fail to see you as you are.

Ah, the distractions of human life.
What does not live within the body
Is but tawdry clothing on a stick figure.

Open

consider things that open
jars windows
lights roads
faucets awnings
elevators wounds
anemones

clouds open for rain
fall on open flowers
doors to neighbors, strangers
and trick or treaters
minds to wisdom
hearts to love

revelations of truth and myth
written on walls, hidden in shadow
behind closed blinds
reveal pathways to
courageous conversion
when they open

contemplate the pill bug
a roly-poly creature
its back crinkled like a lobster tail
touch it and afraid, it rolls into a ball
undaunted and curious, it opens
like an unclenched fist

Jo Ann Smith

Unmoored

today's daylight wind, clocked for its
uncommon speed, blew into my mind
with intermittent fury and parboil simmer
fierce then still, sparked then void
like an old battery firing, but
unable to hold a charge

tossed unmoored in this
gale of knockdown force
building up, bowing down
bounced back and forth in an
unrelenting pattern, leaving
only seconds in an untimed pause

a pause
as faint as an echo
no longer than a sigh
yet long enough to choose
to see windswept trash
or listen for answers in the wind

My Gilded Pony

I am wide awake
behind closed eyes
in a dream state
afloat on a cloud
holding no rain
detached from a
gorged world
determined to
devour itself

far away I hear
a calliope
I think it is
the 4th of July
and I am ten again
inside a rhythm of
hypnotic carousel spin
holding no reins
my gilded pony strains
to pull each down to up

a euphoric moment
of stunning clarity
more transcendent
than aware
immune to the
passing of time
over before indelible
remembered only for
the longing of its return

Oh to Be a Cow in India

in a tiny Hindu village clopping along the streets
among the stalls of squash and eggplant,
the chai wallah refilling cups, as stray cats rush
to lap up the spilled pour, the sweet taste of jaggary
draws a parade of ants to share in the boon;

the shops lined with rows of statues to Shiva dancing
and Durga cross-legged riding her tiger,
saris woven with gold thread hang from racks
arranged by colors bright in the sunlight

a breeze tickles the bells strung across
the spice-sellers doorway —
aroma of cardamom and ginger
scents the air and covers the undertones
of manure and last night's garbage

no need to fear the swarm of people, all vegetarians,
or be concerned about the shouts and screeches of children
against the chanting from the temple
before silence descends for meditation

to roam freely between market and meadow
where the grasses grow near the bathing pool,
a spring of holy water where a guru long gone
healed the devoted, the warm waters now filled with pilgrims
seeking sight or breath or relief from karma's weight

meandering along the path behind the ashram
where the Westerners pray for enlightenment
to find the one who wears the saffron robes
and glides across the open field of cut grass

to meet the eyes that see
the heart's one still flame
everything given in the silence of her gaze
as she brushes her scarf across your head
to scatter the flies.

The Shape of Shadow

fractals bind and shape
the image cast on the trail
where the tracks once rocked
the train to San Francisco

a patchwork trunk steadies
boughs and oblong leaves that
tremble in the breeze

walkers chatter against
the whirr of tires and wheels
spun by cyclists and skaters

we step aside and discover her
reflection on the pavement
look up to find the old oak bent
by sunlight and storm

in silence we walk behind
our shadows long in sun's arc
leading us toward home

Turnings

still life memories arise and shift
the long line of you tucked into the chair
a cup of orange pekoe held close in your
delicate hands, the scent of tea accents
a long-ago story reimagined between sips

the silent flutter of falling leaves
casts stillness over the buzz and thrum
of summer as the light ebbs —
winter's slumber returns

in the corner of a room
resides an empty blue chair
its fabric sun-streaked
with each turning

we held the space of shared history
I now hold, my mind's eye views
a kaleidoscope of turnings until the
images shatter in the silence
I cannot remember your voice

Sleepwalking in Yosemite

New Year's Day
awakens me as I try
to evade the waterfalls
cascading down, loud
by hiding under boulders
that fail to protect me
from freezing water
but the fresh air
reminds me
my morning breath
is horrible
not just to tourists
but to myself.
Via cellphone
I quickly call
my pharmacist
at Rite Aid
in Oakhurst
who tells me
it's the eleventh time
I've called her today
to learn what brand
of toothpaste
she recommends.

Some Thoughts About Heartburn

Similar stories of life
at the local Peet's Coffee
and the local Starbuck's
where managers sternly
ask me to leave despite

the policy of free refills
so my need for caffeine
sends me driving away
until I find myself
inside a Von's Market

where I drink bottles
of Mocha-Frappuccino
as a wandering cashier
simply doing her job
grabs my four-pack

while I eat pills
called Pepto Bismol
to stop the caffeine
from destroying
my stomach wall

and the cashier admits
she loves me but never
will she try Pepto Bismol
because she loves Tums
which I will never try

so we hug each other
for hours in Aisle 17
both of us aware
this is the last time
we will have together.

Problems in Northridge

Go talk to Rachel's friends
says my dad while I watch
my sister's female friends,
all obscenely beautiful
but they don't see me
or hear me coughing
as they parade by me
on their afternoon date
with the swimming pool.
My afternoon date
is the asthma spray,
Proventil
which helps me breathe
as I view a TV movie
about June 6th, 1944,
D-Day
on the Normandy Beach.
The Americans,
despite the slaughter,
push forward
to the beginning
of the end of Hitler
and his goose-stepping,
speed-freak Nazis
while I sit here sad,
anonymously trying
to gain courage enough
to talk to the girls
out for a tan
in the backyard.
There's a documentary

about World War II
on the television
I tell the girls
who quickly
cover themselves
with their towels.
One pretty girl
asks my sister
Who is that weird guy?

A Falcon

He turns his head.
Wraps me in his disdain.
Neither prey nor predator,
not worth the effort.
He turns back.
His still elegance not negating his hunger.
Stillness is necessary for his survival.
A lord of the skies he may be,
but he would not turn down a pigeon for lunch.
That fat one waddling beneath my bird feeder.
And then he is down.
Faster than my eyes can track.
Feathers and blood flying.
The pigeon already a torn carcass.
He finally meets my eyes.
Wary that I will challenge him for his prize.
I do not begrudge him his meal.
Plenty of pigeons, very few falcons.
I retreat into the house.
Leave him to his feast.

Morning Ritual

Today
her son dressed
in worn out blue jeans
just like he likes them,
a red flannel shirt.
Her daughter in black leggings
a laurel-leafed colored
turtleneck that brings
out the green in her hazel eyes.
Each morning
before she goes
to work
iPhone in hand
she takes a picture.

Then she kisses them goodbye.

During lunch
she goes to the corner market
weighs the almost ripe tomatoes
pulls beans off the shelf
gently kneads the avocados
feels her son's cheek in the leathery skin
sees her daughter's smile in the imprint
left by her fingers.

She worries,
as she does every day,
if today will be the day
she gets the call, hears the text alert.
School lockdown.
Ready, armed
with pictures;
she will refuse
to surrender her heart.

It Has Come to This

The moon rises across the valleys of my face
Light catching oranges and yellows
A mid-autumn life soon turning to snow
Looking up at the stars counting the uncountable

Light catching oranges and yellows
Memories falling around me
Looking up at the stars counting the uncountable
Hills and trees trout in the stream

Memories falling around me
A dense thicket of stardust
Hills and trees trout in the stream
Starfish and sand dollars kelp at my feet

A dense thicket of stardust
Cracking the shell of my smallness
Starfish and sand dollars kelp at my feet
Dew drops of angels on blades of grass

Cracking the shell of my smallness
Life soon turning to snow
Dew drops of angels on blades of grass
Moon rises across the valleys of my face

If the Moon Fell

If the moon fell,
what good would it be
just floating a bit offshore,
its unrelenting brightness,
no longer distant,
the entire city sleepless.

Waxing, waning missing,
ashamed of its pock-marked
complexion and lack of
gravitational pull—tides gone,
the shoreline now tiresome
save for the moon's
slightly bobbing presence,
its luminosity no longer having
anything to do with the sun.

Perpetually full, but never
again filled with romantic
notions. The sky is darker,
shadows are deeper,
and sanitation workers
are chipping away to remove
it from the landscape.

Still Life

I am thinking of Henry Moore,
of roots tunneling through stone,
when my chair shifts slightly
when I did not.

To my right,
branches of Meyer lemons
tap at my window,
Dishes in the sink
rattle a little,

but I am not alarmed until
the sudden splash behind me.

A stream is flowing
under the bridge in a painting,
only now it spills over
the edge of its frame.

Leaping up, I grab this
favorite Cezanne off the wall
and rush it outside
to flow into my yard.

I return to the flooded room
and notice another Cezanne
(Apples on a slanted desktop)
whose fruit now yields to gravity,
rolling off, bouncing along the floor
to gather at the front door.

When I let the apples out,
standing before an easel
amid beckoning blooms
of lavender, is Cezanne,
endowing the life of his canvas
with the movement of bees.

After Fran Claggett-Holland

Witness

I flip the seat up
and sit down.
Between my bare feet,
a small dot moves.
It looks confused.

It is black with a red abdomen
and has eight out of sync legs,
like they've never walked before.

A few propel her forward,
others quaver her in a circle.
And although her feet
are on the floor,
she resembles a turtle
on its back.

I blow on her,
but she doesn't leap
or scurry as startled
spiders generally do.

I watch for a while.
Her shuddering subsides,
she folds her legs under her,
and goes limp to one side.

It has been a long time
since I've watched something die.
I wonder if I will be as
confused and directionless,
limp legs curled under.

And will anyone witness my passing?

A Time When

Wait, come back.
Stay with me
Just
A little while.
Embrace me,
Adore me
Like
You used to.

There was
A time when
You couldn't get
Enough of me.
A time when
My absence
Made you cry.

I couldn't wait for
A time when
We'd part ways
With a smile,
For you to
Skip away
Carefree and strong.

But now when
I say goodbye
You reply
"Whatever"
Tone sullen,
Eyes on the ground.

And I wonder
What
I was thinking
Wanting you
To grow up.

Quotidian

In poets' minds, cascades of words
stream into their lifeblood.
Expression waits for an ordinary sound,
a smell, an image to burst forth
onto a white page.

A homeless woman
sits on a curb of a screaming urban
street teeming with life.
Snow falls quiet-like around her;
    nowhere to go.
Twelve stories up, a heated apartment,
a poet watches tragedy unfold,
translates anguish;
Words on a white page, hot with outrage,
unlike cold in a winter storm.

A young woman in red heeled boots,
runs across an urban street,
falls in the path of an oncoming bus.
A poet's hand reaches out,
pulls her to the sidewalk from certain death—
both unnamed, unharmed;
but not forgotten: her brush
with mortality translated
onto a white page.

People find their way through urban streets
to gardens nestled between towering buildings.
Bright gold and orange koi swim in pools
surrounded by flowers and trees and glass;

A poet sits on a stone bench; sees
the overlooked, hears the overheard.
The details of daily life burst forth
onto a white page.

Call It Any Name

Yesterday, I stood in front of a purple Mexican Bush
Sage, though call it any name, call it something
beautiful, call it a color reflecting sunlight, tangible as
the glimmering hummingbird hovering around, whose
harmonic cricketing hum awakened my delight.

I spoke to my companion, "look at the world reaching
out in splendor and celebration. Isn't it grand?"
He cocked his brown freckled head, his amber eyes smiled
assent, his tail wagged, he sniffed the fragrant air wafting.
All of us joined cells; one chimera, a moment in the day.

What I Miss About My Hometown

The way geraniums grow wild like weeds.
The velvet green of the mountains in spring.
The wonder when one can't see outstretched hands.
Reaching sandy shores in ten minutes time.
The shimmering beauty when the sun shines.

I do not pine for silvery cold skies,
or the bone chilling blue Pacific air,
but down here on mornings rare, misty thick
gray hovers amongst the trees evergreen,
and fills me with a deep serenity.

Chernobyl

The half-life of the Cesium-237
Entombed in reactor 4
Is 4 billion years,
Around the same length of time
The Earth has been circling the Sun.
There is comfort in knowing
That in 4 billion years, when the Earth
Is being swallowed by the Sun,
Our signature on this planet
Will still exist, and 4 billion years later,
When the Sun is a burnt-out cinder,
The last of that signature
Will finally fade from the universe.

Ode to the Itch

The Attention-getting Itch
The itch insists that you notice it.
If you resist scratching, the itch persists.
If you scratch, you acquire a scratch plus an itch.
The scratch should be scrapped lest the injury induces infection.

The Unreachable Itch
The itch often taunts me by locating on my unreachable back.
Sometimes I ignore all anti-itching advice and use a Portable
    Extendable Metal Stainless Steel Back Scratcher to scratch the
    otherwise unreachable area.
And sometimes I use a back brush to apply a topical itch-relief
    cream to that tauntingly itchy back.
Anti-itch creams are sensational.

Ditching the Irresistible Itch to Itch
The itch has upgraded its status.
The itch has been elevated to a sixth sense — along with hearing,
    touch, taste, sight and smell.
Science can cure the urge to scratch an itch in mice.
Science may soon enable us to scratch the itch entirely.

Time and Teapots

Some people are frozen in time
Like John F. Kennedy or Marilyn Monroe
Alive back in the 60's
Never to get old

When I left home at eighteen
Cousin Abby was a little girl
Doing the teapot dance
In the living room of our youth

Yet the spell can be broken
Time can race ahead
Just because you didn't notice
The clock keeps ticking

Dr. Abby came to visit last week
With her second husband
And stories of her three adult kids
Time played its game

Crows walked on our faces
What doesn't die young, grows old
Little teapot illusion
Lies shattered on the living room floor

Seems No One Writes a Sonnet Anymore

Seems no one writes a sonnet anymore.
Who shall compare thee to a summer's day?
You'll find no similes or metaphors
except in my sweet words—they show the way.

I want, I need the fourteen metered lines
the A-B-A-B rhyming scheme. No free
verse odes splaying across the page like crimes
of modern art. Such words come not from me.

Your bard of love begs forbearance. Forgive
all my clichés—My love is blind! I am
helpless hoping these honeyed words will leap
straight from the page into your heart and mind.

Today, always, 'til winter's upon us
you'll find my love when you read this sonnet.

Never Lost

Always, when our moon matures to fullness
I sense the cord between us close — You,
first born child, now a man, far from home.
From earliest sight you looked to the skies
where the distance you saw eclipsed my own.

I don't know if that closest orb interests you now.
Though I whisper *goodnight* to you each time
I sense the advent of its comfort, feel its serene light.
Pray for you these nights at winter's peak, to see
our moon in greatest splendor — ripe in possibility.

Replay the words of my last letter, in my mind. Repeat
those wishes I've always hoped for you. Near dawn
I wake to someone knocking in my dream. A cue before
the moon slides out of sight. Your dad wakes me to see
the perfect ball of light through our window from the west.

At once I recognize this moon's message from you.
A response graced with forgiveness — the acceptance
of letting go, letting be. With eagerness I step outside —
to view our horizon without barrier of walls and glass.
The moon — now gone! The cold dark sky, a void.

Bereft, my joy drains, replaced with panic.
How could this be? A sudden rush of wind and cloud?
Did time pass so quickly the wonderous moon has left?
I rush up the steps and back inside. To search again,
to stand right where your parents saw the sight.

And there it is, in former glory. Unchanged, the full ripe
glow—a porthole through a frigid sky. There I see
it was *where I stood* made me think our moon had gone.
Standing low, on the grey pavement outside our home,
I lost perspective to believe all could disappear.

It is time I embrace each appearance,
the waxing assurance, whatever the future-to-be…
You are never lost when I hold the patience to see.

Appendices

Poet Biographies

STEVE ABBOTT has published seven articles about pre-Prohibition Sacramento whiskey dealers and saloons. He has written a song while riding a bicycle to Indiana and lyrics for another for his late wife's 75th birthday. Both are on YouTube.

SUSANA ACKERMAN is a bilingual writer, educator and translator who was born in Lima, Peru. She is a world citizen with a deep love for language, culture and poetry. She has taught Spanish language at Santa Rosa Junior College and has led human right delegations to Central America.

KATE ADAMS is a writer living in Mountain View, California. Her previous work has appeared in *Centennial Review*, *Zzyzzyva* and the *Sand Hill Review*. Poets that have influenced her are Matthew Arnold, Wallace Stevens and Gjertrude Schnackenberg.

BARBARA ARMSTRONG, devotee of the Blue Moon Poetry Collective, is fascinated by the nuanced power of words and their intrinsic music. Her poems have appeared in anthologies and other publications. Her diversions are storytelling, linguistics, Balkan music, gourd crafting, home constuction and organic blueberry farming.

JUDY BAKER'S mission is to help nonfiction authors grow their influence and income. She is co-writing *Cultivate: How to turn readers into heroes, raving fans, and paying clients* and a memoir, *Gratitude Gumbo: Resilience Recipes for Women with Ovarian Cancer.* She resides in Sonoma with husband Garry, and their chickens.

SUCHANDRIMA BANERJEE grew up in the bustling city of Calcutta. She travelled to the United States to pursue doctoral studies at UC Berkeley and settled down in the Bay Area. Suchandrima is a habitual poet and an avid reader. Growing and cooking farm-fresh produce, and woodsy trail-runs keeps her close to nature.

MARGARET BARKLEY is a poet, teacher, and curious observer of humans and nature. Her first chapbook *Ribs* was published by Finishing Line Press in 2021. She has an MA in Psychology with a focus on group facilitation, has taught at SSU and USF, and has led a writing group since 1999.

JORY BELLSEY is a cynic, pondering the incredulity of politicians and wondering who coined the term "alternative truth." Jory writes to make sense of things. He has been published in anthologies.

HENRI BENSUSSEN (she/her) has published poems in *Blue Mesa Review, Common Ground Review, Sinister Wisdom, Into the Teeth of the Wind,* among others; *Earning Colors,* a small chapbook of poems, was published by Finishing Line Press, 2014. She earned a BA in Biology/UC Santa Cruz.

LES BERNSTEIN is an award-winning poet. Her poems have been published in anthologies and journals in the USA and internationally. Her book *Loose Magic* is available on Amazon.

NATHALIA BERNSTEIN is currently in college. Her poetry has been published in Rattle. She loves seeing her poems in print.

AMRITA SKYE BLAINE writes poetry, fiction, and memoir, developing themes of aging, coming of age, disability, and awakening. She has been published in twelve anthologies. She began writing poetry at age seventy and has the practice of writing a poem every morning at dawn.

LAURA BLATT has worked as a website writer, a laboratory technician, and a publishing company manager. Her writing has appeared in various publications, including *Lilith Magazine, The Poet, California Quarterly,* and anthologies produced by Redwood Writers. Now retired, she makes her home in Penngrove, California.

RICHARD BOYD is a retired physics professor with more than 250 publications and books on nuclear physics, nuclear astrophysics, and astrobiology. He has written seven novels, most of which deal with problems he feels are facing modern society. He writes poetry for amusement.

MARIANNE BREMS is the author of three poetry chapbooks. The most recent, *In Its Own Time,* is forthcoming in 2023. Her poems have also appeared in literary journals including *The Bluebird Word, Front Porch Review, Remington Review*, and *Green Ink Poetry*. She cycles, and swims in Northern California. Website: *www.mariannebrems.com.*

NOTTY BUMBO is a writer, artist, and poet in Fort Bragg, California. His work has been published in small journals and presses, including *Telling Our Stories Press, Peacock Journal, Calabash Cadence Taisgeadan, Word Fountain, Poetry South* and others. A novella, *Tyrian Dreams*, is available through Amazon Publishing.

LANCE BURRIS is a fine arts painter, illustrator, and published author who lives in Napa, California. His focus is on local "place settings" and the relationship between poetry, painting, and prose. He believes the poetic spirit underlies all art forms.

CURT CANFIELD graduated summa cum laude from Moravian College with majors in English and History with honors. He retired in 2017 to pursue his interests in religion, philosophy, and modern history and recently completed his first novel, *The Errors of Mankind,* which will be published this summer.

PATRICIA CANNON has been a Registered Nurse at UCSF since 2001. She has worked in cardiac critical care, neurointensive care, hemeoncology, school nursing, and currently, in research. Her passion is her faith, photography, and the written word in all its forms.

FRAN CARBONARO found refuge and a home in Sonoma County in 1976. She holds two BA degrees in Expressive Arts and Theater Arts from SSU. Fran's poetry has been published in various local anthologies. *I'm Still Alive*, a CD of her spoken poetry and song, was released in 2018.

SIMONA CARINI was born in Perugia, Italy. She writes poetry and nonfiction. Her first poetry collection *Survival Time* was published by Sheila-Na-Gig Editions (2022). She lives in Northern California with her husband, loves to spend time outdoors, and works as an academic researcher. Her website is *https://simonacarini.com*

JUNE CHEN has taught in public schools and in community colleges for more than 26 years. She has been schooled in India, Myanmar (Burma), Egypt, Guatemala, and the United States. She currently lives in Whittier, California. *Seeing The Light* is her debut novel.

SUSAN CHURCH DOWNER disliked poetry until recently, dismissing it as too obscure, or too trite or just word salad. She joined a poetry group two years ago to placate a friend and found unexpected joy in the art of choosing words carefully, expressing thoughts economically and riding the rhythms.

FRAN CLAGGETT-HOLLAND a teacher, poet, and sighthound-lover, finds great satisfaction in seeing others' poetry dreams materialize. After a career of high school and university teaching, she traveled widely as an educational and BAWP consultant. Moving to Sonoma County, she taught memoir and poetry for Osher Lifelong Learning at SSU. Fran has published four books of poetry as well as many books about teaching literature and writing. Her latest book, *Under the Wings of the Crow, A Legacy of Poems, New and Selected* (RiskPress), is available from Amazon.

LAWRENCE SHERMAN COHN is a participating member of the California Writer's Club in San Francisco and the Peninsula. He started his career in poetry when he was published in Littack Magazine (William Oxley-Ed) as part of the Vitalist Poetry genre in Oxford, England as well as in various literary journals.

TINA DATSKO de SÁNCHEZ is an author/filmmaker whose poetry films aired on Sundance Channel and CNN Showbiz Today. Her bilingual poetry book, *The Delirium of Simón Bolivar*, won the Phi Kappa Phi Award. *Swimming in God* and *Dancing through Fire* are part of her four-book series of poetry inspired by Rumi and Hafiz published by The Pilgrim Press.

PAUL DeMARCO is a member of SRJC Older Adult Poetry Class. He has lived for 36 years on a six-acre property near Petaluma. He began writing poetry four years ago after retirement from his career in non-profit finance. He is published in the local anthology *Moonlight and Reflections* (2022).

SUSAN DLUGACH taught English in New Mexico and California. She also reported for the Las Vegas Daily Optic while living in northern New Mexico's Sangre de Cristos. *California Update* and the *California Writers Club Literary Review* have published her poetry and articles. Stereotypical poet, she lives with a cat in Sacramento.

CAROLYN DONNELL has been published in anthologies and won awards in fiction, poetry, and memoir from San Francisco Writers Conference and San Mateo County Fair Literary Arts. Also two novels (under C. S. Donnell). CWC South Bay's 2018 Matthews-Baldwin service award and CWC's 2019 Jack London Award. *https://www.amazon.com/C-S-Donnell/e/B017GGDZTI; https://carolyndonnell.wordpress.com*

NANCY CAVERS DOUGHERTY is a writer and artist, and author of four chapbooks with *Heaven is in Truckee* most recently published by The Orchard Street Press. Her poetry has also appeared in many literary journals and anthologies. Originally from Massachusetts, she and her husband live in Sebastopol, California.

PATRICIA DOYNE holds an MA in Creative Writing from San Francisco State. She's a retired teacher, who studies botanical art and performs with Wadaiko, a taiko drumming group. She's President of ART, Inc., Vice President of Pen Women, and Secretary of the Fremont Area Writers.

LINDA DRATTELL's poems, fiction and nonfiction are published in several anthologies, newsletters, magazines, and online publications. Her poetry chapbook *Remember This Day* will be published in August 2023 (Finishing Line Press). Her co-authored children's book *Who Wants to be Friends With a Dragon?* was recently published. Twitter: @LindaDrattell. Website: *www.LindaDrattell.com*.

PETER DUDLEY is an author and executive coach in Walnut Creek. A Cal grad with a long and diverse career, he's proud to be the father of two wonderful adults. His most recent book *together,* a collection of poetry and photography, is available now. Find him at *graybearcoaching.com*.

MARCIA EHINGER, MD a native Californian, is a retired pediatrician and genetic specialist. She has written medical articles, poetry, memoir, historical-fiction and fantasy. Marcia is the past California Writers Club Sacramento Branch newsletter content editor and was included in the club anthology *Visions*.

MAUREEN EPPSTEIN'S most recent poetry collection is *Horizon Line* (Main St. Rag, 2020). She has a new chapbook forthcoming from Finishing Line Press. Her work has appeared in many journals and anthologies and has been nominated for a Pushcart Prize. Originally from Aotearoa, New Zealand, she lives Mendocino CA.

ANITA EROLA, originally from Finland, is a bilingual dual citizen. Her writings have appeared in numerous anthologies. Her photography and poetry have won awards locally and internationally. Anita enjoys travel, especially to Finland when the summer days are long and lake water warm.

REBECCA EVERT is a member of Rumi's Caravan, a Bay Area oral tradition poetry performance group. She considers memorizing and reciting poetry an essential part of her spiritual life. As a member of the Blue Moon Poetry Salon, she also pursues the art and craft of writing poetry. Rebecca is an urban farmer and an avid propagator of bee and butterfly gardens.

YOLANDA FINTOR has been published in magazines and newspapers as a free-lance writer. She has a co-written cookbook, *Souper Skinny Soups,* published by Pelican Publishing Company. Her most recent cookbook, *Hungarian Cookbook; Old World Recipes for New World Cooks,* was published by Hippocrene books, Inc. Several of her stories have appeared in CWC-SFV anthologies.

ROBIN GABBERT has poems in RW anthologies, CWC *Literary Reviews* and *The Best Haiku* 2022. Her *Diary of a Mad Poet* came out in 2020 and a book of ekphrastic poetry, *The Clandestine Life of Paintings, in Poems* in 2022. Her haiku and tanka appear in *Burro in My Kitchen,* published by Blue Light Press in 2022. Robin lives in wine country with her husband Con and pup Hamish.

JUSTIN GODEY lives in Napa, California. In 2011 when his first child was born, Godey realized he could not bear the thought of handing his baby over to daycare. He became a stay-at-home dad. There he learned to embrace his creative side as an author, poet, and songwriter.

JOAN GOODREAU'S recent work includes *Strangers Together: How My Son's Autism Changed Our Family, Another Secret Shared,* and *Where to Next?* She is currently working on poems taken from interviews with parents of autistic children during the pandemic and has exhibited her poem collages.

DEBORAH GROCHAU moved to Woodland, California when her adult children flew the nest. After years of teaching English and history, she is spreading her wings by writing historical novels. A nomad at heart, she has traveled extensively in pursuit of her muse.

CONSTANCE HANSTEDT'S poetry has appeared in literary journals, including *Rattle, The Comstock Review, Naugatuck River Review,* and *Calyx.* She has published *Treading Water* (Finishing Line Press, 2022) and *Don't Leave Yet, How My Mother's Alzheimer's Opened My Heart* (She Writes Press, 2015). She is a member of the CWC Tri-Valley Branch where she leads the poetry critique group. Visit *www.constancehanstedt.com.*

KAREN HAYES lives in Sonoma County. She loves her cat, Healdsburg, Fort Bragg, rivers, and driving. Currently she has one book of poems published, *River Stone.* Now that she is almost settled in a place in Guerneville, after a year of being very unsettled, she hopes to start being productive again.

NATHAN HEGEDUS is a journalist and essayist whose work has appeared in *Slate, Quartz* and *The Wall Street Journal,* among other places. He has written extensively about Swedish paternity leave and other parenting and gender issues. He is now exploring haiku, haibun and other forms of Japanese poetry.

BASHA HIRSCHFELD has been a writer and a seeker all her life. She lives in West Sebastopol and teaches meditation at a retreat center which she developed to give people a peaceful place to get to know their own minds. She finds the process of writing poetry a path to self-discovery.

BRAD HOGE'S 2nd book of poetry, $N = R^* fp \times ne \times fl \times fi \times fc \times L$ (The Drake Equation), is available from VRÆYDA Press. His 5th chapbook, *A Human Lifetime*, is available for pre-order from Finishing Line Press. His poetry appears in numerous anthologies and journals, most recently in *California Literary Review, Faultzone: Reverse*, and *Consilience*.

ROSI HOLLINBECK'S work has appeared in *Highlights, High Five*, and *Humpty Dumpty* magazines and three editions of *Today's Little Ditty*. Her story-poem "The Monster Hairy Brown" was published in *Thynks* (London) anthology 50 *Funny Poems for Children*. She writes book reviews for several on-line reviews and her blog at *rosi-hollinbeck.com*.

JON JACKSON is a retired neuropsychiatrist who lectures on Rainer Maria Rilke, Lou Andreas-Salomé, and the psychology of the Old Testament. He is an award-winning poet. He recently published a memoir of his father's life and a collection of his poems. He lives in Santa Rosa.

KUSUM IRENE JAIN in 2018, as part of her "How Best to Deal with Grief" experiment, where she was both the mad scientist and the guinea pig, found she was able to set her world of science, business and logic aside to connect with her emotive self through her poetry.

MARA JOHNSTONE grew up in a house on a hill, where the top floor was built first. With a lifelong interest in fiction, she has published several books and many short stories. She can be found up trees, in bookstores, lost in thought, and at *MaraLynnJohnstone.com*

KARL KADIE is a poet and author of *Revenge of Nature* and *The Burning House*. His poetry has been published in the Poetry Ink anthology, *Train River*, Redwood Writers anthologies *Beyond Distance* and *Crossroads, The Santa Clara Review, The New Verse News, Haiku Headlines*, and *One Hundred Thousand Poets for Change*.

JUNE KINO CULLEN'S poems and short stories have appeared in *Small Print Magazine, Adelaide Magazine, California Writers Club 2022 Literary Review,* and others. She is currently working on her memoir for which she has received three writing fellowships and hopes to complete the first draft later this year.

ELIZABETH KIRKPATRICK-VRENIOS' award-winning chapbook *Special Delivery* was published in 2016; her second, *Empty the Ocean with a Thimble* in 2021; and her third, *Concerto for an Empty Frame* is due in 2023. Nominated three times for a Pushcart prize, she has poems published in numerous anthologies and journals.

GALE KISSIN is Brooklyn born and California conscious. She finds her life story just beginning to unfold in a poetic voice.

JEAN GORDON KOCIENDA is a former geopolitical intelligence analyst currently working on her first novel, a historical fiction account of the life of Japanese feminist poet Yosano Akiko. She regularly posts new poetry translations on Instagram (@accidental_feminist_tanka) and Facebook (*www.accidentalfeminist.net*). Jean is a Board member of CWC Marin.

MARGARET LANGE is a poet, writer, singer/songwriter, storyteller, and voiceover artist from Nipomo, California. She is co-editor of *Imprints,* an ezine of the Coastal Dunes branch of CWC, and she serves as an arts commissioner for Santa Barbara County. Previously, she taught poetry workshops to students with California Poets in the Schools.

CRISSI LANGWELL is a romance author with 13 published books, but only dabbles in poetry. She joined Redwood Writers in 2012 and has served as past prose anthology editor. Currently, she is the club's vice president, newsletter editor, web editor, and social media manager, and was this year's recipient of the Helene S. Barnhardt award. Find Crissi at *crissilangwell.com.*

SHAWN LANGWELL is the Immediate Past President of the California Writers Club (CWC), Redwood Writers, past president of Toastmasters of Petaluma, an inspirational speaker, and top producing media salesperson. He is the author of the memoir *Beyond Recovery: A Journey of Grace, Love, and Forgiveness* and the recent release, *Ten Seconds of Boldness: The Essential Guide to Solving Problems and Building Self-Confidence.* You can find Shawn at *www.shawnlangwell.com*

PATRICIA LeBON HERB is an Objibway Indian, American, Belgian, Mother, Wife, Painter and Poet.

GEOFFREY LEIGH has taught and conducted social science research, has published articles and co-edited a book, *Adolescence in Families.* He lives in Napa Valley and works at a local winery. He published a non-fiction book, *Rekindling Our Cosmic Spark*, a novel, *Dancing with Audacity,* and *Prosetry Journey* with co-author, Marianne Lyon.

DOTTY LeMIEUX has had five chapbooks published, her latest from Main Street Rag Press, entitled *Viruses, Guns and War.* In the 1980s, she edited the literary magazine *Turkey Buzzard Review.* Her work has appeared in numerous publications. Her day jobs are running political campaigns and practicing environmental and tree law in Marin.

BETTY LES writes about the intersection of science, nature, and the human condition. Favorite themes are birds and insects, the deep presence of rivers and trees, and the consciousness of rocks. Betty was chosen as a Redwood Writers Award of Merit Poet in 2018 and is a member of the Blue Moon Poetry Collective. Her Chapbook *Just Enough to See* was published by Finishing Line Press in 2023.

MARIANNE LONSDALE writes personal essays, fiction and poetry. She's looking for an agent for her novel *Finding Nora*, a story set in Oakland in 1991 about love and friendship during the AIDS epidemic. Her work has been published in *Literary Mama, Grown and Flown, Pulse* and several print anthologies.

SHERRIE LOVLER is a painter and poet from Santa Rosa. She is an Art Trails artist and teaches painting classes online and in person. Sherrie's paintings and poems inspire each other and are paired in her award-winning book *On Softer Ground: Paintings, Poems and Calligraphy. ArtandPoetry.com*

ROGER LUBECK is president of the California Writers Club. He is a past president of Redwood Writers and president of It Is What It Is Press. Roger has published 11 novels, two business books, two dozen short stories, a dozen poems, and two performed short plays.

STEVEN LUBLINER is the author of the political satire *Threeway,* and the Hanukkah memoir *A Child's Christmas in Queens*. He is also a prize-winning poet, two-time Redwood Writers contest winner, and anthologized author. His short plays have been performed by the Raven Theater, 6th Street Playhouse, and the Petaluma Radio Players.

CHARLOTTE LUCEY is the author of *Air Borne,* a collection of her poetry. She has a Master of Arts in Creative Writing from San Francisco State University. She also writes fiction and enjoys astronomy and nature. Charlotte served on the Board of Directors of the Marin Poetry Center and is a member of the Marin Branch of the California Writers Club.

MARIANNE LYON has been published in various literary magazines and reviews. She has been nominated for the Pushcart Award 2016. She is a member of the California Writers Club, Solstice Writers in St. Helena California. She is an Adjunct Professor at Touro University Vallejo California. She was awarded the Napa Country Poet Laureate 2021 title. Co-authored *Prosetry Journey — Exploring Expression of the Heart* with local writer Geoff Leigh.

ELAINE MAIKOVSKA is a retired lawyer writing in Petaluma, California. Her work has been published in *The Coachella Review, The Medical Liability Reporter, 95% Naked,* edited by Daniel Coshnear, Redwood Writers' *Vintage Voices, the Argus Courier,* and the 2021 and 2022 Redwood Writers poetry anthologies, as well as *On Fire,* the 2022 RW prose anthology.

KATHLEEN McCARROLL MOORE is a poet and children's book author who served as the Poet Laureate for the City of San Ramon for three consecutive terms. She has published two poetry collections and two middle grade novels; her debut picture book will be published in 2024.

MEGAN McDONALD was named Literary Stage "Exhibitor of the Year" at the San Mateo County Fair in 2018 and placed in that contest's poetry division in 2019. Her poem "Firebrands" appeared in *Fault Zone: Reverse,* and her poem "Burn Scar" earned Honorable Mention in the 2023 Redwood Writers contest.

BRIAN McSWEENY'S seven lifetimes: family trauma (Ouch), childhood star scholar-athlete (Yay), Stanford bound (Standing ovation), college dropout down and out (Bummer), Tibetan Buddhist devotee (What?), Men's work-therapy-Eros (Finally!), Raising autistic son and Special Ed. teaching (Digging deep), and lucky seven, Retirement and the Writing Life (Follow your Bliss).

JOANNE ORION MILLER is the author of seven destination guides (five for Amazon Travel, two for other publishers), multiple non-fiction articles, one historical novel *Shaketown: The Madam's Daughter,* and an upcoming suspense novel *Power Lessons.* Her story "Penance" was short-listed for the Raymond Carver award. Joanne Orion writes poetry in the middle of the night and throws it in a drawer to ripen.

HILARY SUSAN MOORE is a founding member of Off the Page Readers Theater, which has included her poetry in several performances. Hilary began writing poems as a teen, and most recently was published in Redwood Writers' *Beyond Distance* and Phyllis Meshulam's *The Freedom of New Beginnings*.

DONALD NEEPER grew up in the southern Colorado mountains. His scientific career at Los Alamos, NM focused on solar buildings and environmental restoration. After retiring to Portola Valley, he wrote one novel and is now developing a popular-level book on American anxiety as seen through the lens of complexity.

PAT OBUCHOWSKI believes that the greatest invention of all time is the invention of language. She is a Leadership Coach and has authored/co-authored four books on playing your bigger game. She is a world traveler and a newly self-declared poet. A new and exciting journey for her.

BOB OKOWITZ grew up in NYC. The best part of his youth was being on the high school swim team. He loves to laugh. He got a BA in English in 1970. Ten years later, Bob had become a social worker, got married and started a family. Twenty years after that, Bob joined CWC/SFV and got back to writing.

NATY OSA divides her time between Chico and Mendocino and is a proud member of the Writers of the Mendocino Coast. She's been published in the WMC and the CWC anthologies.

JOAN OSTERMAN lives in Napa, where she explores the magic in everyday life through poetry, memoir, and fiction. Her work has been published in The California Writers Club 2022 *Literary Review* and several Napa Valley Writers anthologies. She presents her poetry at venues throughout the Bay Area.

PAMELA PAN is an English professor at San Joaquin Delta College where she teaches writing and literature. Pamela's work has been published in magazines and anthologies. She writes poems, fiction, and nonfiction. Her current project is a historical fiction based on her grandma's life during WWII when Japan invaded China.

AMY PANE lives in West Sonoma County at the edge of the Laguna. Her poetry has appeared in the Redwood Writers anthology *Crossroads*. She is currently writing poetry and memoir.

CAROLYN RADMANOVICH felt compelled to write her first book, after a near-drowning incident on the Russian River. *The Shape-Shifter's Wife* was a winner of the 2018 Independent Book Awards. In the sequel *The Gypsy's Warning,* Heather time travels in search of her sister, and finds love and adventure in 1849 San Francisco.

DIANE RAWICZ reads and writes poetry to experience the mystery and magic in its precision. She feels that poetry breathes life into the simplest and most complex thoughts. When writing her memoir becomes too demanding, she turns to poetry. Diane is the editor of *Write Angles*, the CWC-Berkeley weekly newsletter.

CHERYL RAY has published magazine articles, including *Sail, Latitudes & Attitudes, Writers' Journal,* and *Spirited Voices.* Also, essays were published in *The Girl's Book of Friendship, Elements of English,* a 10th-grade textbook, and the SF-Peninsula CWC *Fault Zone* anthology. With her husband, they have sailed over 30,000 nautical miles.

LINDA LOVELAND REID is Past President of Redwood Writers, an author of two novels, and a Jack London Awardee. Linda teaches art history for SSU and Dominican Universities in their Osher Lifelong Learning programs. She is a figurative and abstract painter, has directed community theater for 30 years, and serves on several Boards of Directors. *www.lindalovelandreid.com*

MARGARET ROONEY has been published in several RWW anthologies, *The Ekphrasis Journal, The California Quarterly, The Blue Unicorn, Reverberations,* and several other poetry journals and magazines. She won First Prize in The Redwood Writers Poetry Contest and two of her poems were nominated for a Pushcart Prize in 2020. She has a chapbook *A Wild Rain* coming out in 2024.

SHANTI ROSENBLATT is a free-range yogini. Her poems have appeared in journals, anthologies and presses. Her poems are vegan and gluten-free.

CAMI RUMBLE lives in California's Central Valley and her roles include wife and mom to two kids as well as Chief Operating Officer of the house. This COO enjoys reading, writing, sewing, and connecting with friends. She strives to approach life with truth, openness, faith, and practicality.

ERIN SCHALK is a writer, visual artist, and educator living in Orange County. She has been published in Northeastern University's *Pensive,* Schoolcraft College's *The MacGuffin, Wales Haiku Journal, The Petigru Review,* and others. Schalk is also the author of (quiet, space), a book which combines her poetry and visual art.

BART SCOTT is a Petaluma-born street lawyer living in Santa Rosa. He has been scribbling since he was a kid, a long time ago. He also plays guitar and sings, primarily songs consisting of three chords and some speculation.

JO ANN SMITH'S career in public education culminated as a high school Superintendent. In that capacity, her writing relied on the orderly left side of her brain. She now finds herself drawn to the reading and writing of poetry — a creative journey that continues to be challenging and liberating.

LINDA STAMPS writes poetry and fiction. Her poetry is published in a variety of anthologies including *Phoenix: Out of the Silence, Pandemic Puzzle Poems,* and *Reverberations: A Verbal Conversation.* Haiku, tanka and haibun inform her writing. Her novel *Laid to Rest,* about a woman obsessed with funerals, remains in process.

SCOTT STRUMAN has been writing poems for 25+ years. His poems have been published in *The Northridge Review, The Moorpark Review, Spillway* and *Jewish Currents,* among others. Scott grew up in Northridge, CA. He has taken poetry writing courses at Cal State Northridge, Fresno State and Moorpark Community College.

LINDA TARRANT is a new member and is looking forward to the camaraderie and support. She has been writing seriously for the last five years and is in the process of finding an illustrator for the children's book she has just finished and will publish — one way or the other.

WINDFLOWER TOWNLEY lives with her wife on the Mendocino Coast in Northern California, on unceded ancestral land of the Pomo people. Her poetry has been published in numerous journals and anthologies. A book of her poems will be published in February 2024.

STEVE TRENAM teaches poetry writing for Santa Rosa Junior College. Blue Light Press published his *An Affront to Gravity* last year. His work appears in *Pandemic Puzzle Poems* and in the ekphrastic poetry book *Canyon, River, Stone and Light.* He is a founding member of Poetic License Sonoma.

CHARLOTTE TRESSLER grew up in North Texas but escaped to Northern California in her teens. There she found fellowship, a fella, and raised a family. Her writing is centered around family dynamics and often includes animals.

BILL TRZECIAK has written plays, stories, humorous and political poems he calls doggerels, readers theatre scripts, columns, and novels in between his life work as a librarian, actor, and teacher. His trilogy saga fantasy of a disabled magical librarian in a world of evilly divided culture is his current project.

JUDITH VAUGHN lives in Sonoma, California. She is a member of Poetic License Sonoma and Redwood Writers, a branch of the CA Writers Club. Publications: *First Literary Review-East*, an online literary publication, '20-'22; *JerryJazz Musician*, several online collections, 2020-2023 *Crossroads*, Redwood Writers' 2022 poetry anthology; *Moonlight & Reflections*, Valley of the Moon Press 2022; and Larry Robinson's *Poetry Lovers*, 2022

ANNE MARIE WENZEL was born in San Francisco and is an economics graduate of San Francisco State University. She has studied creative writing through Left Margin Lit and Stanford's Continuing Studies. Her poetry appears in *Humble Pie*, the California Writer's Club 2022 *Literary Review*, and the forthcoming *Fault Zone: Detachment.*

STEPHEN WILHITE has spent most of his life dabbling in poetry with little conviction that he could become a serious poet. He received his M.A. in English from CSULB and taught English for a few years before embarking on a long career in workplace learning. He currently lives and works in Vienna, Austria.

MICKIE WINKLER is the author of *Politics Police and Other Earthling Antics* (Austin Macauley 2020), She is billed as an irreverent writer of short humor and poetry. Her stint in politics, and as mayor of Menlo Park, CA. inspired her humor. "Humor," she says, "was her alternative to despair."

ROBERT NATHANIAL WINTERS joined the Navy from NYC. The Vietnam veteran earned his BA from Sonoma State College and a masters from CSU Stanislaus. He has written a variety of books. Bob lives with his wife in the Napa Valley. Despite having Parkinson's disease, he writes almost every day.

NANCI LEE WOODY was a college professor and textbook author before writing her award-winning novel *Tears and Trombones*. She recently completed the Pilot episode to convert the novel into a streaming series for TV. Her short stories and poetry have been widely published online and in print anthologies.

JAIME ZUKOWSKI'S poems are published in *Canyon, River, Stone and Light*, 2021 *Blue Light Press;* Redwood Writers poetry anthology *Crossroads*, 2022; *Moonlight and Reflections*, 2022 and *Sonoma Sonnet*, 2023, Valley of the Moon Press. Jaime also presents her work at virtual poetry readings with Sebastopol Center for the Arts.

Artist's Statement: Sherri Loveler

Sherrie is both a painter and a poet and combines the two in unique ways.

She fell in love with calligraphy from the moment she held her first broad nib pen in a high school art class in the Bronx. That path led her to study with many world-class calligraphers and she became well known in the field herself.

Art has always been part of Sherrie's life, encouraged early on by her parents. Writing poetry has come in and out of her practices, but it, too, has been with her since early days. It was when these two disciplines found each other that she finally had purpose and meaning in her work.

Sherrie says, "Now, instead of writing words with my pen, I paint the movements and gestures of calligraphy with a brush. This change has brought about an Asian look to my work. I usually begin with ink, with a mark that resonates with a particular poem. Water is an important element, as it adds fluidity and an uncontrolled aspect to my painting. I keep the poem in mind and will read it as I paint, letting it inspire me. These paintings are not planned; they become a dialog with what is on the page and what wants to come next. The result is not an illustration of the poem, but an abstract painting that embodies some aspect of it. Not all my paintings stem from poems and many poems don't have paintings. I try to hold all this loosely as I allow the work to grow and change over time."

Sherrie has a BA in Studio Art and currently teaches abstract painting online as well as in person. Her book, *On Softer Ground: Paintings, Poems and Calligraphy,* won Most Outstanding Book Design of the Year (2016) from Independent Publishers Book Awards (IPPY).

www.artandpoetry.com

Redwood Branch History

Jack London was first attracted to the beauty of Sonoma County in 1909, the very year he was named an honorary founding member of the Berkeley-based California Writers Club [CWC].

In 1975 Redwood Writers was established as the fourth CWC branch, due to special impetus from Helene S. Barnhart of the Berkeley Branch, who had relocated to the North Bay. She and forty-five charter members founded the Redwood Branch of the CWC.

Redwood Writers is a non-profit organization whose motto is: "writers helping writers." The organization's mission is to provide a friendly and inspirational environment in which members may meet, network, and learn about the writing industry.

Monthly meetings are open to the public and feature professional speakers who present a variety of topics on writing techniques, publishing and marketing.

The club sponsors a variety of activities, such as contests, workshops and "reading" salons. Over a dozen writers conferences have been held, offering seminars on various areas of writing.

Each year, Redwood Writers publishes two anthologies with prose and poetry, giving members an opportunity to publish their work.

An extensive monthly newsletter and award-winning website, along with other social media outlets, keeps members in touch with one another, to share accomplishments and successes.

Redwood Writers is indebted to its founders, to the leaders who have served at the helm, and to our many members. Without this volunteer dedication, Redwood Writers could not have developed into the professional club it is today with over 250 members. For more information, visit *www.red-woodwriters.org*.

Redwood Writers Presidents

Redwood Branch is indebted to its founders, members, and to the leaders who have served at the helm. Without their volunteer hours and dedication to the club's mission, Redwood Writers could not have developed into the professional and successful club it is today with over 300 members.

1975	Helen Schellenberg Barnhart	1997	Marvin Steinbock (2 years)
1976	Dianne Kurlfinke	1999	Dorothy Molyneaux
1977	Natlee Kenoyer	2000	Carol McConkie
1978	Inman Whipple	2001	Gil Mansergh (2 years)
1979	Herschel Cozine	2003	Carol McConkie
1980	Edward Dolan	2004	Charles Brashear
1981	Alla Crone Hayden	2005	Linda C. McCabe (2 years)
1982	Mildred Fish	2007	Karen Batchelor (2 years)
1983	Waldo Boyd	2009	Linda Loveland Reid (3 years)
1984	Margaret Scariano	2013	Robbi Sommers Bryant (1.5 years)
1985	Dave Arnold	2015	Sandy Baker (2 years)
1986	Mary Priest (2 years)	2017	Roger C. Lubeck (3 years)
1988	Marion McMurtry (2 years)	2020	Shawn Langwell (2 years)
1990	Mary Varley (2 years)	2022	Judy Baker
1992	Barb Truax (4 years)		

Awards

Jack London Award

Every other year, CWC branches may nominate a member to receive the Jack London Award for outstanding service to the branch, sponsored by CWC Central. The recipients are:

1975	Helen Schellenberg Barnhart	2003	Nadenia Newkirk
1977	Dianne Kurlfinke	2004	Gil Mansergh
1979	Peggy Ray	2005	Mary Rosenthal
1981	Pat Patterson	2007	Catherine Keegan
1983	Inman Whipple	2009	Karen Batchelor
1985	Ruth Irma Walker	2011	Linda C. McCabe
1987	Margaret Scariano	2013	Linda Loveland Reid
1989	Mary Priest	2015	Jeane Slone
1991	Waldo Boyd	2017	Sandy Baker
1993	Alla Crone Hayden	2019	Robbi Sommers Bryant
1995	Mildred Fish	2021	Roger Lubeck
1997	Mary Varley	2023	Crissi Langwell
1998	Barbara Truax		

Helene S. Barnhart Award

In 2010 this award was instituted, inspired by Redwood Writers' first president, to honor outstanding service to the branch, given in alternating years to the Jack London Award.

2010	Kate (Catharine) Farrell	2018	Malena Eljumaily
2012	Ana Manwaring	2020	Joelle Burnette
2014	Juanita J. Martin	2022	Crissi Langwell
2016	Robin Moore		

Additional copies
of this book
may be purchased at
amazon.com.

Made in the USA
Las Vegas, NV
22 September 2024

95666694R00148